Anthony J. Peter

D0317134

How To Become
Financially Free

A personal finance handbook
showing you how to end
financial and employment insecurity

Copyright © 2010 Anthony J Peter

The moral right of the author has been asserted.

Apart from any fair dealing for the purposes of research or private study,
or criticism or review, as permitted under the Copyright, Designs and Patents
Act 1988, this publication may only be reproduced, stored or transmitted, in
any form or by any means, with the prior permission in writing of the
publishers, or in the case of reprographic reproduction in accordance with
the terms of licences issued by the Copyright Licensing Agency. Enquiries
concerning reproduction outside those terms should be sent to the publishers.

Matador
5 Weir Road
Kibworth Beauchamp
Leicester LE8 0LQ, UK
Tel: 0116 279 2299
Fax: 0116 279 2277
Email: books@troubador.co.uk
Web: www.troubador.co.uk/matador

ISBN 978 184876-389-0

British Library Cataloguing in Publication Data.
A catalogue record for this book is available from the British Library.

Printed in the UK by MPG Biddles, Kings Lynn, Norfolk

Matador is an imprint of Troubador Publishing Ltd

How To Become Financially Free

Australian born Anthony J. Peter began his career as a Chartered Accountant in 1982 working the next 27 years in that profession in Australia, Holland, and Germany. As Partner he advised hundreds of companies and individuals on over 150 national and international company take-over transactions at times worth billions. At 48 he left the fast lane of business to realise his dream of becoming a Writer in the world of private finances.

To my children "Annika and Stefan" that they have at least some insight into what their father did during their early lives, the time when I spent less time with them than I realised and wanted. More importantly though, I hope that they learn from my experiences, both good and bad, and the lessons I learnt forming the foundation of my own personal freedom at age 48, which hopefully will help them in an ever unstable world.

To my mother and father who gave my brothers, sisters and I an indestructible foundation in life through a perfect upbringing. On financial matters I will always be grateful to my father who's basic financial philosophy was brilliantly simple, and was a key driver in my own financial strategy.

Last, but certainly not least, to my dear wife Beate who not only had her time fully occupied with the family, but who also always found the strength and time to be my loving partner, my sanctuary always providing refuge against an ever-aggressive world. This book is for you Beate, and our "little island world".

1

Contents

Introduction

The idea of this book is to transport my private financial codex and financial lessons of life into a form that will be of interest and will help your own financial freedom. Of course "freedom" means many things, but I have chosen one aspect which I enjoy writing about. One always tries to pass down learnt wisdom, this usually happens after the first blunder has occurred. The wise words may, or may not, fall on receptive ears and they may, or may not, be remembered. Often they bring something only after repeated blunders and when a particular, shall we say "maturity threshold" has been reached or passed. None the less I wished to document my experiences, observations, adventures, blunders, lessons learnt, and particularly the simple rules of a private financial codex in this book. They have all led to my personal freedom, something truly valuable. I dearly hope the same for you!

Author's notes
This book represents a compilation of personal views on private (largely) financial matters formed via wisdom passed down, as well as personal experiences over many years. Although financial strategy and selected investment subjects are presented they are all done so in the form of private opinion only. This book is not to be understood

as a recommendation for the purchase or sale of any form of investment asset class whatsoever. The reader is solely and fully responsible for their own financial and related strategic decisions, the suitability of which are, and remain, as individual as the reader. Any form of liability whatsoever cannot and will not be taken on by either the author or the publisher.

The denomination of currency has been left neutral in this book. All examples using money were originally euro denominated.

July 2010

1
Why?

Why? Why this book?

Too often have I heard the frustrated longing for freedom and independence from friends, family and especially my (ex) colleagues. People locked into their jobs, locked into the need for that monthly pay cheque, locked into the worry of losing that job, who are enduring the silent contained panic of having to drudge through the years to make that company pension scheme, pay down that mortgage. They are hopeful to get the funds together, to sufficiently supplement whatever form and amount of pension they will (hopefully) one day receive. Maybe this sounds familiar? If you're 40 plus and happen not to be one of those well paid managers of the enterprise elite, you may be *one of those* ageing and greying, drudging day in and out, losing sight of life outside work as it passes ever faster by. A life spent not stopping to ask if you're planning to partake, but rather ignoring you, writing you off, because you are too deep in your path to get out, like the "living dead".

This book is focused on two groups, (1) the younger workforce (say up to the mid-30s) including those about to enter the workforce, and (2) those moving close to the 50s caught in the middle as it were, those with a limited future career time frame not looking at a secure, timely retirement.

For the 1st group, their future is now marked by the greatest period of financial and economic instability since the Great Depression, not to mention ever present and rising geo-political instability, coupled with ever growing global environmental threats. In addition, the globalization of markets has created opportunities for industry, and for those equipped with the right skills and flexibility to continuously adapt to work changes, often involving work beyond one's own borders. This environment is also helping to drive evolutionary shifts in economic power from more traditional economic centres to rapidly rising new players who will gain influence and domination over the next years. We must add to the ever changing, or should I say mutating, macro and micro environments, the fact that job security and continuity is fast heading toward extinction. Such extinction needs to be accounted for in the light of the dying (or largely already dead) opportunities to benefit from company retirement schemes and, subject to the national social security systems in place, as indebted government support for an ageing population evaporates.

For the 2nd older group the story is similar except the level of skill and job flexibility tends to decline with age, even if savings positions and pension rights tend to compensate. One could say that for the people in this group who have saved, who are truly secure in their jobs with a low risk perspective, who have a pension outlook, their strategy to independence and freedom will be different than their younger counterparts. Needless to say, those older people who are not so "privileged", are in the poorest of situations. However, no matter what your situation, this book will provide guidance and support to financial freedom!

What does this all mean for those with a good portion of their work lives still ahead? Becoming independent and free of work and financial worries will be one crucial factor to your quality of life, your health and your happiness! The responsibility for this will rest solely with the individual, *you*, because no one is going to help if you fail this objective.

So, who am I? Someone who has been through the "rat race" over the past 3 decades, active in the world of finance, company deals and accounting in 3 countries, over 2 continents, and who has experienced the joy, and indeed pain, of starting from the bottom as a photo copying graduate and fighting through to being a Partner in a "big 4" public accounting firm. I have been involved in Corporate and Private Equity take-over transactions over the past 13 years, covering over 150 company take-overs. I have had the "pleasure" of hundreds of observations of business colleagues, friends and acquaintances, many whom I (not disrespectfully) term the "Living Dead". People trapped in jobs or careers, too scared to change, or who can't change, scared of their ability to "hang on" long enough to reach illusionary financial independence or make it to that long desired retirement at 60 something, although the big "finish at 50" is their dream, at least according to countless discussions I've heard over the years. People who, if they "make it", will be zapped of the greatest part of their lives and who may, or may not, enjoy their post zombie lives for a shorter span of time than envisaged. Thanks to some passed down financial wisdom and some golden rules, which I only learned to really value and appreciate after passing 40, was I spared the living dead fate.

These often sad observations have fascinated me for many years. No wonder really, when one sees live horror scenes of the future self, the "worst case scenario", sending cold shivers down the back, you tend to do a lot of thinking about how to avoid the horror show. In my experience, such thoughts tend to start from about 38 and increase in intensity over subsequent years. As far as I could tell the great majority of those I observed didn't think of ways out, instead they forced themselves to give only brief attention to their current situation, believing that they could not leave the only path they were acquainted with. A path leading down a deepening trench, ever more impossible to escape, heading to their "made it" or their "worst case", but in either case heading to de motivated frustration, (often unfair) disgust of their employers and organisations, greying, ageing and becoming shells driven only by their "have to" rather than their "want to".

For those of you who belong to the 2nd (older) group who are happy in their job and who don't earn the label "dredger", the issue is less acute, at least let's say healthier. If you belong to this group and also have your financial future secured and sewn up then you probably don't need to read any further, that is, if! Things can always change of course!

This book will give guidance on the steps needed to become financially free and independent over time, as quickly as possible, because speed will be of the essence. A handful of key principle rules will be presented and explained, practical tips given and tools suggested all to provide a practical and easy guide to help you achieve your freedom. This book will also take you through some personal financial reserve building strategies, the mechanics thereof and effective approaches to the discipline and continuity that will be crucial in winning your independence and freedom.

I actually decided to write this book for my children Stefan and Annika before they finished school, and before they started their careers. The basic idea was why should they not have the benefit of my 3 decades of experience, at least in theory? Without sounding like "the old guy", I admit a challenge, wouldn't it be great to give them some advice on their work and financial futures which, even if only placed at the backs of their minds, would help steer their future. Apart from this ideological motive there is a very real need to share knowledge due to the ever more brutal future they face when it comes to their post-work situation. If I can also share this with other readers along the way, it'll be an added bonus!

My motivation is not just the desire to help others prepare for their later lives and live without the shackles of job and financial dependence, but the observations mentioned above have also caused concern and sympathy for my former colleagues frustrated anger and disappointment at what seems to be an ever encroaching system of repression of those who need to serve, in contrast to the few but ever more powerful being served. Don't get me wrong, I am pro-free enterprise, but I also believe that working life should be motivating, rewarding and embody respect and self esteem. It is these crucial elements which are under threat for many.

A fascination for (and the deep study of) macro economics (while not ignoring the political developments) has allowed me to form some conclusions on the longer term trends I believe we'll be facing in the future, and which will be impacting the financial and job security of the majority. Macro economic theory and statistical data interpretation is not the focus of this book, none the less here is a selection of personal observations and views on some longer term key trends. (I apologise that some understanding of macro economics is helpful for a few of the comments below).

> Significant difficulties in the rebalancing of the world's surplus vis-à-vis deficit economies as well as continuing financial industry / markets risk for the real economies, all feeding economic disruption and continuing boom / bust cycles.
> A continuing rebalancing of living standards between developed and the so-called emerging or developing economies.
> Ever increasing commodity and environmental costs.
> Slow (stealthy) stagnation or decline of real living standards in a number of key developed nations for ever larger portions of the workforce as these nations are forced to continue competing against the rising mass powers in the East.
> For a number of key developed nations deteriorating government fiscal positions (debt) and the continued demonetarisation (inflation) of their currencies.
> Continued expansion of the gap between the developed nations, wealthier minority and the broader working majority, increasing downward pressures also on the classic middle classes.
> Growing low wage / temporary work encroachment into the traditional (higher cost) full and longer term employment areas.

> The continued encroachment and standardisation of multi-job existences.

I could continue but have objectively tried to extract some of the developments which I believe warrant serious concern. All of the above spell the opposite of long term job security. In fact they confirm the likelihood of the creeping stealth repression of increasing cross sections of society.

I always felt closest to those "not in power", despite my belonging to the other group for the last decade. As described above, I firmly believe there is a need to support all who feel trapped, used, or lacking in financial perspective, and most importantly those feeling insecure and hence not free. This book is the most effective way I believe I can help!

Before we move onto the next chapter a word on something of great importance to me, namely independence. What does this have to do with this book, and any future works I may write? Writings on financial matters are often tainted or skewed by financial investment bias, often to the potential disadvantage of the reader. There are authors who may have set views or vested positions who are still able to write objectively, I am personally grateful of such works, especially over the last few years! There are however authors who often have alternative sources of income, be it from the financial press, their own advisory practices, or from financial institutions, and so on. They may hold significant holdings in the stock market, commodities, or other private forms of investment. Such positions held by authors may influence their leanings, intentionally or otherwise. Being an old school Chartered Accountant I have always focused on being without bias in the advice I have given to many hundreds of clients over my professional career. This will also be the case in this book. One function of independence is mind-set and character, the other of factual vested interests. I consider myself to be truly free and independent of income sources I can't 100% personally control, and this is actually the goal of this book for you! Conservativeness I'll admit is my middle name, although I try to keep an open mind to all forms of investment, those I understand, and those I don't, are viewed 100% neutral; not to be promoted, nor to be condemned. This book deals with financial planning strategy and an attitude focused on winning financial independence and freedom by building the base financial resources needed (savings), not with investment strategy or forms of investment promotion which are a subject of personal preference and competence. There is more than enough material available elsewhere on the latter. I do however provide some personal views and strategies in the supplementary chapter of this book, which you may find of interest.

The financial aspects to gaining independence and freedom are not the sole key drivers to a happier life, they are however gaining weight in a world ever less tolerant and forgiving of those who don't plan their personal freedom early in life.

If you want to know more about me and why I wrote this book, my own personal motivation for (financial) freedom and the path I took, you can read more in the appendix. For those of you about to start, or still forming your careers, there are also career experiences and corresponding (sometimes painful) lessons about what I learnt included. Otherwise in the following chapters we'll get on with your own freedom plans.

2

Defining "financial freedom"

This sounds like a straightforward question, one which encourages an impulsive response and that everyone should have an answer to. I didn't find it easy, not one bit!

I guess "freedom" is relative to one's own life situation. There are also different types of freedom; health for someone taken ill, solitude for those continuously in the public eye, asylum for one unlucky to be born into an unfortunate country, something as "simple" as the well-being of one's child. The list of examples could be as long as there are people in the world.

The focus of freedom in this book relates to your private financial world, granted not the key aspect of life by any means, but an area deeply relevant to most. Ring fencing the area I am talking about helps us qualify the question which now reads "what's the definition of financial freedom?" As mentioned, the answer may not be that easy to find. There will be no one answer that fits all definitions, there may be, at most, a grouping of similar answers which will apply to certain groups of people in similar financial, career / work, family situations. To illustrate some of the factors influencing your definition here are some examples of different situations:

➢ Someone with a net financial worth of X or more million (the original currency denomination euro has been neutralised throughout this book) may yearn for an extra Y million "to be truly safe and free" of financial worry, to win financial freedom – I doubt however that such a person will ever realise true personal freedom in this case...

➢ A janitor may yearn for 5 to 10 thousand to finally give him some breathing space in the bank account, make that overdue car repair, or take a break after 15 years without a holiday...

➢ The factory worker or tradesman may basically want job stability, satisfaction and security; if this could be permanently realised financial freedom may then exist. Such a status quo for the rest of one's working life is a rarity these days, hence this person may define financial freedom as an undefined sum of money, in an undefined form and over an undefined time period...

➢ A public servant with a job that practically can't be axed (also an ever-shrinking minority) may have reached his or her financial freedom. Sometimes they may think about an undefined safety-net sum which would be nice to realise travel dreams or just to act as a "rainy day" fund in case of the unforeseen...

➢ The athlete may realise there is only a limited career span to become "established", a time line where the need to earn well, as long as he or she still can, will dominate, because the earnings situation after one is "over the hill" can't be predicted. Financial freedom for this person may well be

more demanding and extreme, it could mean setting aside
enough financial resources to survive the post-sport career
where possibly no earnings will follow...

➤ A single office employee may define financial freedom and
true luxury as 100 000 or a little more without any real
thought behind the sum in focus. The parent with 3 young
children will surely aim higher, but then again the extremely
vague "whatever" amount will receive little serious thought.
There's just too far to go, and the "whatever" definition of
freedom is unattainable anyway. So why bother...

This list can go on, for each individual there is a story and personal
universe which will lead that individual to define their personal
make up of whatever their financial freedom could be.

In this book I would like to place a simple caveat on any forthcoming
definition of financial freedom, the definition should be a realistic
and reachable one. Yes it won't be financial utopia, but a realistic
goal. That goal will not be something one may achieve "at the end.
Who knows what might happen before the end is nigh. The
definition, and goal of realising that definition, should be achievable,
let's say by the "mid-point". In terms of the achievability in a given
time frame we want this to be motivating also!

In terms of preliminary logic, this book may exclude two groups
from its discussion, namely those public servants who may be super
secure, and those swimming in wealth. Otherwise we'll be focusing
on the broader majority, albeit that is still very wide indeed (this does
not mean that this book isn't relevant for those "excluded", they may
not automatically feel financially free!). If you belong to the other

groups, either directly or sub-consciously, I'll bet at some time, either regularly or spontaneously, you have asked yourself "how's my financial security...?" Such thoughts will vary in frequency, depth and seriousness depending on factors such as age, personal character, responsibilities, job situation, etc. Generally the older one gets and the higher your commitments or responsibilities, the more serious and frequent the thoughts will be. Those who don't care, who think along the lines "I can't change anything anyway so why worry", or "why should I bother about the future at my (young) age", and even "by then (60) I'll be dead anyway", could be said to enjoy a relaxing philosophy of life, but such cool dudes still need to sustain a roof over their heads, food, life's basics, health care, etc... until they're (most likely) well into their 70s 80s or maybe further.

You can come up with your definition of financial freedom, I explicitly encourage this as focus and goal setting is the 1st step to achieving something. If you just bumble along without giving thought to what you really want to achieve, not making that a goal, logically that end point will not be reached. No matter what your definition of financial freedom might be, whatever your financial goal may look like, let me suggest 2 definitions which should fit or integrate with any individual definition:

Definition #1
The ability to financially survive without your current income for 1 or more years.

Definition #2
The ability to be financially independent of any organisation for the foreseeable future.

Both definitions will be the subsequent focus of this book. Definition #1 is the broad spectrum goal of financial freedom that will be achievable for the majority of you. Definition #2 relates to financial freedom relevant only for a minority, but is also one which finds its place later (chapter 5) because it is so often sought, pondered upon and dreamt of!

I personally find the two "freedom definitions" present a useful contrast to each other, thereby helping this discussion. The first entails the practical aspect of building a "rainy day" reserve for the unforeseen and future retirement needs, but in my view helps relieve and hopefully abolish psychological pressure from your current working environment. Number one is there to present a counterbalance to those threats that may play on your mind like job security or job satisfaction, or the ever growing future risks that may plague you (unbeknown as they may be at the current point in time). You could say that number one is the "everyday" freedom solution for the majority. The second definition is for the most a dreamer's solution of freedom that is normally not achievable now, nor soon, and has a long term character. It may however be within reach for more people than first thought. In aiming for number two one will automatically pass through number one in any event.

So, number one is very simple, it's the peace of mind of knowing that no matter what happens with your work or within your life generally, you at least have the financial firepower to survive for one or more years, usually more than enough time to get back on your feet and protect your hard earned standard of living, assets, and family. As the reserves in number one grow, so too does the level of financial freedom or independence. You're no longer trapped in the

.ger exposed to unforeseen threats that could de-rail se dependent on you, you become increasingly free and re... .ctually you'll most likely experience a side benefit as well, the more relaxed you become the more creative, liked and productive you'll also be within your work and at home. I'll even go so far as to say that you'll have a positive double spin effect, the first definition financial freedom supporting your work so that you won't even need the reserves you've set aside. The reserves will just grow and support you and your dependents in your later life, supporting private planning for retirement which is becoming more vital by the day.

I mentioned at the beginning of the book that the primary purpose for writing it was to pass certain valuable life lessons to my children. The simple definition of freedom (number one) was also passed down to my brothers, sisters and to me from our father. He always stressed that we should strive to have one year's pay in the bank as soon as possible, i.e. as a matter of priority. He noted that once you've got your year's pay in the bank you're free to fulfil your job as you see right, you're no longer, or significantly less a slave of your firm or boss, less of a forced "yes" man, of which I personally have seen way too many over the years. He would note that this financial reserve was for his peace of mind as it enabled a solution to his ever repeated question that one should always ask "what's the worst thing that can happen?" This question applied to all facets of life, not just the financial or work side of things. The answer in this specific financial / work case would be that you could lose your job. This, however, is not such a big issue because you've been prepared for just such an event, you have your comfortable financial reserve to carry you over. With somewhat admittedly macabre humour my father would also add his famous statement that I'll never forget; "..

you then have a year to find new work, that's a lot of time, and, if you can't find work by then, well then you're useless anyway.

Since these words were spoken the world hasn't become more stable! The need for (and common sense of) the number one freedom definition is more relevant than ever!

The following chapters deal with assessing your own financial situation and future, the rules to financial discipline and achieving your own financial freedom. We also take a look at the much pondered upon "how much do I need?" question which analyses both number one and two definitions of freedom and how to get there. Later I'll present some useful simple tools you can use at your discretion.

Before we move on, how about a short look into your financial future?

3

What's your "Relative Wealth" and financial future?

One thing that has always fascinated me is the thought or approach to what I call "Relative Wealth". You are as wealthy as you feel at any one point in time. This feeling will be driven by any number of factors, possibly pure ignorance, but more likely it will be a factor of current and future expected earnings, accumulated wealth, debt and financial commitments, expected or hoped for windfall gains, wealth in a hard measurable form (e.g. cash, bonds, etc) or wealth in an unrealised form (e.g. paper profits on property, shares, etc) and so on.

An absolute key factor to measuring wealth is by comparing what you need to live, survive and enjoy your personal level of comfort to the resources you have and will be earning. Those who live prudently in thrift have a lower wealth requirement threshold than those who squander, or put more politely who need a "life of luxury". These factors are relevant for your own financial future and the question of how you will be financially positioned over time. They also determine the relative wealth you will need to reach your own financial freedom. Taking the above thought further, the amount of financial resources needed to achieve financial freedom, both definitions 1 and 2 from the previous chapter, will vary from person to person. The belief that one needs "x" amount (often implicitly a million in terms of dollars, euros, etc) before one can be considered financially free or wealthy is, I believe, a misguided idea, usually one that develops via "common opinion" and without any serious thought process. I came to realise this via two experiences which had a lasting personal impact.

The first experience concerned an internal administration manager who I greeted every now and then at work. Over the years we didn't just say "hi" in passing but also stopped to have a chat, I guess because I found him very friendly. As time went on I came to learn that he increasingly didn't get along with his immediate boss, slowly but surely his level of frustration grew, it grew to a point where he became trapped and miserable. However something changed in his last year at the firm. He became noticeably more relaxed and radiated a sense of freedom. One morning we crossed paths and as so often in the past, we stopped, putting the routine hectic aside for a moment, to chat. After a few moments he grinned and announced that he was now 50 and would be leaving the firm. I cautiously smiled and asked him if it would be appropriate that I congratulate him. He replied with a warm "yes", explaining that he always wanted to stop work at 50 and that the time had come. He explained that he (and his wife) had sold their house, exchanging it for a boat which was to be their future abode. They planned to sail to the countries and continents of their dreams. He was, it appeared, free. This certainly impressed me, particularly because I knew that he was not a high-powered professional but rather a mid-tier administration manager, who normally would not be in situation to be able to afford this. This experience stuck with me, it got me thinking.

The 2nd experience took place some years later. One of my partners, who I came to know somewhat better via joint projects, didn't really fit the typical scheme of many of us in the firm. He wasn't into expensive cars nor boats, was not a golfer, dressed like anyone on the street, and was not wealth / money possessed. I later found out that he was once a 1960s/70s hippy. He was happy with his hippy apartment and, as it turned out, very simple lifestyle. Like a bombshell he announced in passing during a joint project that he was quitting. He had run up 10 years as a partner and it was now time to call it a day, that 10 years at our position in the type of work we did was the limit. It was obvious that he had clearly defined his formula for freedom, planned it out and was about to put his well calculated and timed relative wealth to full use. For me this was a reminder of my first experience some years earlier. I had nothing but respect for my colleague.

In the two cases above we are not talking about millionaires. Rather people who had apparently assessed their relative wealth quite well and who had also clearly found their definitions of freedom, successfully aligning the two, to move into new phases of their lives. These events and the simple financial life wisdom of my father triggered a thought process that would occupy me for years to come, a thought process combining what the various aspects of freedom meant and what it could take to realise such freedom. One of these aspects is a financial one; one that I firmly believe can be used by the majority of people, including you.

So with the thought of relative wealth in mind let's take a look at the factors that will impact your financial future and hence also your relative wealth going forward.

The factors impacting and defining your personal relative wealth now and in the future can be simply separated into 3 key blocks:

➤ Current net wealth = your current status quo or starting position.
➤ Wealth builders = future net regular income (usually out of employment) and income from investments.
➤ Wealth destroyers = future outlays and obligations.

Next we'll discuss the 3 blocks in principle and provide guidance to assist you in collecting, measuring and calculating your own personal current net wealth and project your net wealth into the future. Moving forward I recommend you first read the discussion on the 3 blocks, taking time to consider your own personal situation in each case and how you will best be able to collect the information you'll be needing later on. Think also about how you prefer to set up your method of recording your data. Suggestions will follow concerning what items you can or should think about, how to best group or classify certain types of data, and how you can present collected data to support the clear and understandable calculations that will follow.

Current Net Wealth

List what you currently own. I'm a financial conservative so what I recommend may or may not always be greeted with approval, but let's say it's a personal "safer approach" to things, especially after the Great Recession starting late 2007! A by no means exhaustive list you can use to get going follows:

- "Cash" (commonly as deposits with financial institutions)[1]
- Receivables (e.g. government treasuries, corporate bonds, etc)
- Other financial investments (e.g. shares, indices, precious metals, etc,) – best valued at the lower of cost or market value[2].
- Current surrender value of insurances from which you expect pay-outs (e.g. capital life policies, capital accident policies, etc).
- Property[3], again at the lower of cost or estimated market value.

Less:

- Debt (mortgage, credit card, consumer finance, overdrafts, taxes due to authorities, etc).
- Other forms of financial obligation, such as leases, which you have entered into to acquire durables such as cars, white goods, TVs, etc.
- Private debt you may have to friends, family, etc.

1　"Cash" in the form of deposits with financial institutions represents in effect a receivable against or loan to those institutions!

2　You may decide to use current market values, if so I suggest only doing so where you plan to sell and realise these values at relative short notice, i.e. where the risk of material falls in the values is low due to a short time frame.

3　Primary owned residence and other owned property

The resulting balance from this exercise, if **complete, accurate** and **honest** is your personal balance sheet of current net wealth. It's your starting point from which you will be able to calculate your estimated financial future and future net wealth.

Wealth Builders

I can imagine many reacting to this block with a somewhat sarcastic grin, ".. there's not much to add here just my sad monthly pay, well what's left of it ....". This may be the case but let's leave any negative emotion aside and list some of the wealth builders that may be relevant:

➢ Your regular net (after tax) income out of employment or similar sources.

➢ Other forms of regular income expected with certainty, e.g. government grants and benefits that are known and secured.

➢ Any expected inheritance – I urge conservative reality here in terms of chance, timing and amount. If you have any real doubt about any of these factors it'll be best to leave this aspect to a "pleasant" (not macabre) surprise whenever it may occur and keep it excluded from any calculations. Or, you engage in an open dialog on the matter with that person(s) from whom you expect to inherit, whether this be appropriate, possible or acceptable will need to be judged by each individual. One could say that the more significant a potential inheritance may be for your financial future (not meaning from wealthy to wealthier) an open and well meant dialogue on the topic could bring significant additional, shall we say "comfort" into the equation.

➤ Any other one-off gains to your net wealth that you can fully bank on, e.g. tax refunds, earned and confirmed bonus payments, etc.

➤ Income from investments held – again I urge conservatism, i.e. the inclusion of only sure and known income which you can bank on, such as interest income on secure receivables and deposits, dividends at reliable track record levels, etc. I don't recommend the inclusion of non-realised gains in investment market values, as such gains can turn sour as the last Great Recession has proven[4].

After collecting this data you will have two forms of wealth builders, regular or recurring items and those of a one-off nature. The same will be the case with your wealth destroyers. As such the presentation of your data will best be on a time line basis. We'll come to the best way to present and process this data later but for now I suggest we first stick to collecting our facts.

Wealth Destroyers

This will probably be the more complicated block and one requiring the most attention, accuracy and honesty. It will also be the block where most discipline will be called upon later in this book. The term "destroyers" has been intentionally chosen, not to sound depressing

---

4   A possible exception will be expected gains from a planned short term sale on what could be considered a steady investment. In such a case a safety buffer deduction would none the less be wise.

or morbid but rather to emphasize the need to realistically measure and control your costs. To make things easier I'll just refer to costs moving forward.

As mentioned above there are 2 types of cost we need to measure and capture, those "regular costs" of everyday life (e.g. food, power and utilities, insurance, transport, etc) and those which are of a "one-off" character that have more of a lasting nature or at least will be rare in frequency, I'll call these "irregular costs" (e.g. vehicles, furniture, white goods, etc).

Regular Costs

What sounds straightforward, and is straightforward, can nontheless be a challenge to list, measure and gauge. Speaking from personal experience it took me weeks to accurately understand measure and track my own regular costs. Upon subsequent reflection this was because I never really paid detailed or serious attention to the matter. Sure, I had a pretty good feeling of our cost blocks and especially what we could or could not afford at most points in time, but being honest, a concerted exercise to accurately document, track and measure such costs had not really taken place. Some years ago I decided I wanted to aim for my own financial freedom and hence unavoidably came to this first task. To help you here are my experience based suggestions on how best to go about listing measuring and understanding your regular costs:

➢ List the costs you regularly have to pay.
➢ Make a distinction between those costs which are deducted from your account automatically and those you pay at

discretion with cash, credit card, cheque, etc.

➤ Concerning discretionary costs for groceries, entertainment, outings, etc you'll need to apply honest actual average experience values. These amounts should be reviewed and adjusted closer to reality over a number of weeks of observation and tracking.

➤ Check your numbers with your latest bills, account deductions, etc.

➤ Make sure you list also the less frequent but still regular items which may be bi-monthly, quarterly, yearly, etc.

➤ Include irregular items such as birthdays, Christmas, etc.

➤ Run through your bank statements, vouchers, insurance policies, and other records to identify costs you may have forgotten. You may be surprised what comes to light!

After this exercise you will have achieved a major milestone.

The next step is to process this data into a useful form. I suggest matching the period of costs with that of your income, i.e. if you get paid on a monthly basis then it'll be most practical to present your costs on a monthly basis. This will require that you calculate all costs into a monthly rhythm, e.g. weekly costs multiplied by 4.3 (i.e. 4.33 X 12= 52 weeks for the year), or quarterly costs ÷ 3, yearly ÷ 12, and so on.

This type of an exercise can be easily processed using a PC program such as Excel but can also be manually set up on paper. Here is an example to help you visualise a monthly presentation of income and costs, we can call this your own personal "Income and Cost Analysis":

Monthly Income V's Cost Analysis

	Actual Status	Potential Reductions	Net after reductions
Joe Blogs (example only)			
Income:			
Monthly Employment Pay (net after tax)	**3200**		**3200**

Monthly Costs :	Actual Status	Potential Reductions	Net after reductions
Health Insurance	500		500
Heating Oil (3800 litres every 18 mths)	127		127
Council Rates (water, waste, taxes, .. @ 465 per qtr.)	155		155
Insurance (see right table)	201	50	151
Telecom	20		20
Media - internet, etc	34		34
Fam. Mobile phones	26		26
Bank fees	7		7
Power (104 every 2 mths)	52		52
Charity	25		25
TV fees & cable	34	17	17
Car #1 - (2X fuel per month)	100		100
Car #2 - (1 tank per month)	80		80
Weekly cash 300 for food, clothing, entertainment, ..	1300	217	1084
Car services (x2 annually @ 600 each)	100		100
Tuition costs	162		162
Non insured medical costs	99		99
Pocket money kids	70		70
Mthly Buffer for gifts, unforeseen, etc	100		100
Total Mthly Expenses	**3192**	**284**	**2908**
Monthly Surplus / (Deficit)	**8**		**292**

Insurances & taxes	
	350
Car 1	390
Car 2	690
Fire	146
Storm, etc	263
Third Party	200
Legal	226
Other	148
Total	2413
Mthly	201

The above is just an example, by no means complete nor the best, but it's an extract of a model I personally use with example content. It took about an hour of bank account statement and other document research to get the numbers together. It did however take time to accurately evaluate the real average weekly cash spent for food, clothing, and entertainment. The table ignores other forms of income, e.g. from capital investments (interest, dividends, etc) or one-off windfall financial gains as well as other forms of irregular costs. These other income and costs are best dealt with separately when we plan and analyse your net wealth into the future.

It might be useful to run through the individual items thinking about their applicability to your own case, adding or deducting items as relevant, and thinking where you'll best be able to extract your own cost data. In the case above for instance there are no residence rental expenses as the roof over the head is paid off. Were this not to be the case rental cost or mortgage interest and principle cost would have to be inserted, and if you are renting council rates and some insurance costs may fall away. In any event it can be an enlightening experience when you first perform this exercise; you may also experience the odd surprise!

Such an exercise is also useful when you need to perform a focused review of the types and levels of costs you incur. You may discover, especially after talking to others around you and from various forms of research, that you have untapped savings potential. There are ample books and literature available on the topic of cost control and reduction. Some of the classic areas involve insurance, subscriptions, transport, and that weekly cash (meaning not just cash but credit / debit cards and similar). I'll be expanding on these later in chapter 5. Cost saving achievements can be deducted from the original costs. Such achievements may not be realisable at short notice but with an improved focus towards cost saving you'll be amazed at what's possible. For this reason I keep the "potential reductions" column active as every pound, dollar, euro, or whatever your chosen currency is, is one extra for your financial reserves and freedom.

It goes without saying that the more you have your regular cost wealth destroyers under control, and hopefully increasingly below the level of your regular net income, the better your ability to add to your wealth going forward will be. If you have the chance to earn more that'll also be great, this is however not always possible, but the opportunity to control and manage costs is always available.

In the case above some limited (not the full amount possible) cost control led to a monthly saving of almost 300 per month. This equates to over 3 400 per annum, or say over 20 years close to 70 000 nominal ignoring interest and cumulative interest effects. Investing these savings with the power of the interest multiplier say at a return of 5% will achieve a financial reserve of around 120 000. In other words, with a little methodical discipline, focus and financial goal setting you can achieve a lot. I'll go so far as to bet that those who don't undergo such an exercise will not only end up with no such reserves after their 20 years but will also have missed other financial potential.

Irregular Costs

These are costs which are incurred or can be predicted / estimated with a frequency longer than one year. Those irregular costs which you know you are about to incur or have become committed to should be listed, valued and then deducted from your net wealth if this hasn't already been done earlier in this chapter. The types of items we may be talking about could be:

- ➢ A replacement or 1st time vehicle.
- ➢ That long planned dream holiday (beyond the "regular cost" norm).

> ➤ Longer term usage items for the house that have become due (white goods, computers, TV, furniture, etc..).
>
> ➤ One-off educational costs, courses, etc.

There will be other items, but all share a common trait to warrant their being deducted from your net wealth, namely:

> ➤ They do *not* add *long term* value to your net wealth (in their own right).

Typical purchases belonging to this category will be cars, all white goods, trips, etc. Logically this includes all items *not* of a true investment nature which don't generate income and wealth in their own right or at least maintain their value over long periods of time (shares, property, precious metals, etc..). If you know or suspect that you'll be spending money on non-investment type items soon (within say twelve months) I recommend you list these, value them as best you can and deduct them from the net wealth balance. Also list expenditures you expect or can estimate over the next years, these will be needed for your net wealth projections into the future.

In this chapter we've concerned ourselves with collecting your financial data, measuring your net wealth and those items which currently promote or build wealth and those which reduce or destroy wealth. We are working on nothing other than your financial status quo. Changing this status quo for the better, managing it to achieve your personal financial freedom are matters we deal with in chapters 4, 5 and thereafter. The status quo or current net wealth you calculated earlier may warrant revision after your review of your costs and documents. Maybe you discovered hidden one-off assets or liabilities correcting your net wealth? If so make any corrections necessary to obtain an accurate picture of where you stand today. Once all of this is completed you should have a fairly good idea (and the accompanying tables) showing the information needed to know your current status, but also crucial to project your net wealth into the future:

➢ Personal net wealth.
➢ A list of your regular investment income.
➢ A list of your one-off or irregular wealth builders.
➢ A list of your irregular costs.
➢ Personal income and cost analysis.

Projecting Your Financial Future

Before you start to project your net wealth into the future the first question will surely be "over what period of time?" There is no single "correct" answer to this. You may have the desire to know your estimated net worth say in 5, 10, 15 or 35 years. You may wish to know the result say when you reach 50 years of age, that being your desired age when you will stop working and turn a new chapter in life! The time period over which you'll end up projecting your financial future will most likely have a strong link to your earlier definition of what financial freedom means to you. In any event I suggest you perform your projections over a number of interim periods or milestones just to raise your awareness of where you'll be over, for example, intervals of every 5 years on the way to your own personal financial freedom goal. You may have multi-financial freedom definitions, interim freedom goals such as achieving 1, 2 or

3 years income in the bank and maybe even the total financial independence definition of freedom. If this is the case simply set your projection of net wealth time frames accordingly.

All financial things being equal (i.e. no financial crises, accumulated wealth maintaining its worth position, etc) projecting your financial net worth into the future can be straightforward. The following simplified path summarises the essential idea;

Current Financial Net Worth

Add: regular estimated investment income (p.a. X number of projection years)

Add: any known and certain irregular wealth builders (within projection period)

Less: any known irregular costs (within the projection period)

Add / (deduct): surplus / (deficit) from your personal income and cost analysis (for each year over your projection period)

= Your projected net worth @ day/mth/year

In the above exercise some elements are, shall we say, more solid than others. The current net worth should be solid if you've been **conservative and honest**. Depending on how you've invested what you may have in net worth, projecting your investment income may be possible. If you've largely invested in fixed interest bearing term deposits, bonds to maturity, etc, then estimating the investment income is a fairly simple math exercise, if however you've invested in shares, investment funds etc, the natural volatility of these make a projection more difficult. None the less, a conservative lowest case historical performance can be used. I recommend an emphasis on "lowest case" past performance and that you keep in mind that outright losses are also possible!

Irregular wealth builders and or costs will not logically enter your projections unless you're quite certain of their amount and occurrence. Concerning the wealth builders, such as inheritance, the emphasis will be on certainty of occurrence *and* amount. If there is any uncertainty I suggest you leave such items out of your projection. On the irregular cost side conservatism is also warranted. As an example, you may not have planned the purchase of a replacement vehicle over the next five years, this doesn't mean you shouldn't plan in such purchases. If your car is 8 years old and has 250 000 miles or kilometres on the clock I'd recommend projecting a replacement within a realistic time frame. The same applies to all essential or desired consumables.

Projecting your personal income and costs should also follow a conservative path. All else being equal, i.e. you stay in your current line of work, you maintain your current lifestyle and associated cost structure, tax levels remain steady for you, you can take your personal income and cost analysis result and project it across the period to which you want to calculate your net wealth. Known and certain changes on the income and or cost side should flow into the projections, but again the elements of certainty of occurrence *and* quantification should apply. Concerning inflation I suggest you simply assume that your income will approximately move in line with inflation, balancing the general cost of living increases into the future (if not, then you can inflate your cost of living over the projection period at your national average inflation rate).

Your projected financial net worth
vs. your financial freedom goals

Now for one of the first tests or moments of truth! Match your projected positions of net wealth over your milestone periods with your personal financial freedom definition(s). If they're on track then you can have confidence in your planning, if there's a negative mismatch of your freedom goals not becoming reality then a "change of strategy" will be necessary. Either way your awareness for the likely outcome of your financial future will have been brought to the surface. You'll now have transparency of where you're headed (in a financial sense) if you simply keep going, regardless of if you have or had a strategy or not. I have met many people without a focused strategy and certainly met many who don't know their likely financial position in the future. Some have vague strategies of just keeping going, maybe making that next promotion, maybe with a key financial goal of paying their house off, but beyond this they usually can't detail anything more certain regarding strategy. I've also met others who do have goals and a strategy beyond that just mentioned, some seem on track and have given their strategy good thought, most however unfortunately have not.

The key point of this exercise is to look into your financial mirror, to realise where you're headed, to realise and look into your financial truth. Once you've managed this you will have achieved another major step towards realising your personal financial freedom.

In the next chapter we'll work on the strategy and game plan to make sure you can achieve your financial freedom goals, irrespective of if you had a mismatch above or not. At this point in time we, or better still you, have set and defined your personal financial freedom, you've collected, analysed and structured your financial data, you've calculated your financial net wealth status quo, and you've projected your financial net wealth into your personal future time frame. Now it's time to improve your future net wealth and to achieve or indeed exceed your freedom goals!

Enjoy entering into the pro-active phase of successfully managing your own financial future!

4

The 10 golden rules that lead to your (financial) freedom

Before we get into a very crucial part of the book, I have a short reflection to make, one driven by two sad events that occurred in my peaceful picturesque village in Germany.

Most people's reaction to financial books is boredom. Maybe with some reflection you'll follow me and disagree? Money management is and can be very emotional. Just recently I was asked to help a family living not far from me. The call for help arose because they knew I was professionally qualified in dealing in financial matters, and knew that my personal management of money wasn't too bad. What I discovered was indeed heartbreaking. After an hour's chat with someone about to lose their house and engage in a double personal bankruptcy (a mother and her son) I was shocked and amazed, later I was also saddened. That same evening I had to write down the emotions they had described. I had to do this to get it out of my system and to have a chance at some sleep that night. The emotions I observed were:

Wrecked, lost, exhausted, scared, angry, frustrated, hope drunk, reality lost.

The text I jotted down went like this:

I have the feeling of deep despair, that educated and intelligent people, people of age, experience and maturity can actually drive themselves into the ground, not in days, weeks or months but in a straight line over years. To a point where there is no turning back, no repair, no "plan B" but just despair and broken wills and the desire to give up, sell up and resign.

Just a week after the experience above another event shook our village. One morning about 10:20 am I heard an incredibly loud bang, one so loud that I first thought that the construction crew on the other side of our valley were having to blast to make way for new foundations. After less than 10 minutes I noticed a huge amount of black smoke spiralling into the sky from the village centre. Upon closer inspection an old Tudor house was in full flame, it was terrifying and sad. The sirens rang without abate, it was like an old war film, the village was shocked and you could feel the fear in the air. I speculated, the affected house was the one for which a public foreclosure notice had been served, basically an open invitation to all to join an auction being held by the bank, an auction to sell a home usually at 70% of the market value, and failing the 1st auction attempt, then at 50% market value.

It didn't take long to hit the news, it even made the national papers. No wonder, a mysterious house explosion doesn't happen every day, especially one involving death. Sadly my speculation turned out to be right. The owner of a house about to be foreclosed couldn't take the shame and burden, this feeling likely being more pronounced in a generally conservative country.

These two local and sad events left their mark on me; they took place while I happened to be writing this. Indeed, money matters can be very emotional and are too serious to be taken lightly or with a sense of indifference!

Moving on to the title of this chapter I'll get right to the point and first list what, for me, have been the golden rules to financial freedom. Nothing mind boggling or scientific, just plain common sense that reads incredibly simply. It's a list which needs to be rediscovered in a large part of today's advanced economic societies. After listing the rules, or codex, I'll then explain what each means in practice. Amongst others, my key personal financial golden rules are;

1. Set your own personal financial freedom goal(s) and time frame(s)!
2. Never spend more than you earn!
3. Live comfortably, but simply, spend only on things you need, and don't show your wealth!
4. Save regularly, set savings goals, also forced ones (ref. I), save any extra cash / earnings!
5. Avoid consumption and speculative debt like the plague!
6. Don't invest your savings in things you don't 100% understand and can't control / manage!
7. Never risk money you can't afford to lose – don't lose!
8. Protect and insure yourself (and family) against major unforeseen risks.

9.   Pro-actively plan for your finances when you (plan to) stop work!

10. Always ask yourself "what's the worst thing that can happen?" and plan for it – have "plan B" ready!

1.   Set your own personal financial freedom goal(s) and time frame(s)!

It might seem strange to have this as the 1st rule but I am a believer in setting goals. If you don't have something you take seriously to aim for you won't achieve it, it's as simple as that.

Earlier in chapter 2 we discussed two broad definitions of financial freedom, the financial reserve of one or more years net pay in the bank, and the more ambitious version of total financial independence. We need to keep ourselves rooted and take it one step at a time. This is why you will have a number of financial freedom goals during your working life time. Your first goal should be to achieve one year's net pay in the bank as a matter of absolute priority! I personally think this goal is also a priority over owning your first house, which is not a bad goal, however it does not achieve financial freedom because it ties up money in an asset and is usually mortgage debt financed. So if something goes wrong with the job, or risk hits you causing a financial loss, your mortgage loaded house won't help you, it may just do the opposite! A self "owned" house is not only the 1st, but also a key and often only solid goal that most have. My personal opinion is, don't follow the majority like a sheep, set your own 1st financial freedom goal with a solid emphasis on winning that financial reserve to give you peace of mind.

Once you've achieved your 1st goal (e.g. one year's pay in the bank) you'll be happier and more relaxed. As is common with human nature you'll also want more after experiencing your 1st big achievement. Goal number 2 will be on the cards. Goal number 2 and potential subsequent goals will be something for your own personal design. You may want to buy your own house, you may want to achieve 2 or 3 years net pay in reserve. Your next goal(s) will depend on your style and weighting of emphasis on how you want to live. Influencing factors will include family, your job and position security, future outlook, etc. In my own case I had the privilege of being in a very solid profession, young, working with a firm almost as solid as the government itself, and had an outlook which could only go up. In this situation goal number 1 was the one year's banked pay, number 2 was our own house (coinciding with our 1st child and the end of our partying 20s), with the subsequent goals numbers 3 to 5 focusing on building the reserves with increasing velocity as the savings potential grew. I started however with goal number 1 and took it one step at a time not aiming too far too fast. Steady consistency is a recommended virtue!

One word of caution however; you can have your financial freedom goals but don't overdo it! Your 1st goal and any subsequent ones should be worked on in a relaxed and realistic manner suited to your own circumstances and pace. Don't forget that the purpose of life is not just living for money, the path to your financial goal should run silently in the background, one could say automatically.

2.   Never spend more than you earn!

It sounds simple, and even naive but it would appear that this is a rule that has been disregarded in western society today.

Indeed one of the key factors leading to the recent Great Recession was over leverage of the private households. It's no secret for instance, that overall (exceptions exist of course) the average US household has spent more than it earns for approximately the last 20 to 25 years. Debt (or leverage) being provided via ever cleverer consumer credit models, the wide spread usage of multiple credit cards per household (often replacing cash transactions close to 100%), and the use of multiple mortgaging to supply debt on the basis of rising paper wealth of house market values, to mention just some of the main causes! Personally I find such a development illogical and dangerous! I hope that the Great Recession, which was on the edge of becoming a full blown depression and meltdown of financial markets and only starved off via international government action on the backs of the taxpayer, forces a long overdue return to thrift and common sense! I'm sceptical however, especially when the proclaimed solution to the crisis from government and leading authorities has been the provision of more credit to fuel more consumption, and this despite receding real earnings power and rising unemployment!

This simple rule is often laughed at and for many has a slight negative and, uncool image. It is however a rule which, although simple in principle, has become clouded in its perceived necessity and application by society through a number of factors.

Some of these factors could be; a less disciplined financial upbringing by the baby boomer and subsequent generations who have had it too good, by consumption driven madness sponsored by a better professional top line (sales) driven industry, and by the providers of the fuel (credit) to feed the consumption madness, namely the finance and consumer products industry. I found that it was getting more and more difficult to keep the discipline of this rule running in day to day practice, slowly and deviously the wish for that consumption "kick" eroded the household financial discipline so that although we never spent more than what was coming in we were often way below our savings potential.

When it became clear that my family and I had to aim for and achieve our financial freedom, sooner than later, the focus on this rule was shall we say "re-discovered"! It became obvious that the good old fashioned household cash book was needed. I didn't want to set up a book tracking cash in and cash out every day, item for item because doing so is an administrative pain and can be time consuming. Instead I developed a very visual and practical tool to track and budget weekly and monthly cash flows, I've named this the "Cash Dashboard". This tool will be fully explained in chapter 6.

3.   Live comfortably but simply, spend only on things you need, and don't show your wealth!

Following on from the above, amassing ever more goods, gadgets, prestige objects, multiples of things we already have beyond true needs, is illogical and a simple waste of your hard earned money. I'm not saying that we should live like say 200 years ago, indeed life should if possible be comfortable, but why that definition of "comfort" should for the majority, mean more than two cars (of which at least one is debt financed) and of a class well above their earnings realm, or a TV for nearly every room, or ever more electronic gadgets, etc, into an endless list of consumption madness, is honestly beyond me. Maybe many in society have lost the true meaning of life, family, friends, love, for the religious (myself included) God, and other things money just can't buy, things where material wealth actually plays no role. This is not a book on the more important things in life; it's about a rather unimportant thing which we need to survive – money. It's a pity that many have lost their focus. The unfortunate thing about money is that if it's not managed well, or indeed mismanaged, it can cause a lot of misery and unhappiness. Hence my conviction in the need for this book.

We seem to be trapped in a society absolutely possessed with the obsession to accumulate as much material wealth as possible, only then to blow it as stupidly as possible. Earnings are made, then blown to such an extent that even more has to be earned to cover our consumption addiction; it seems to me that ever more people are becoming consumption junkies and are heading into their own long term financial ruin without having a clue as to what's happening and the consequences. It also sadly appears that those largely affected tend to be the last generation, although the baby boomers are also well, shall we say, infected. I suspect that the causes for consumption addiction are many; maybe a breakdown in values, flawed upbringings, maybe that consumption itself is increasingly being used and confused as a means to making life meaningful? I also suspect that industry lies behind a lot of the imbalance we now face. Again, I'm all for free enterprise, but I have been active in the big wheels of industry and finance long enough to know that their God is only one, money, and nothing else. I suspect that industry has become too good and professional at enticing common folk to consume at levels well beyond their needs and, to a point, I consider it to be detrimental for society and our environment.

The real problem with this rule is that, for those who are addicted, adhering to the rule will mean the need to become "clean", turn the rudder around, become free of the urge to always consume beyond their true needs. Indeed it'll mean a change in lifestyle and the view of what's important and what's not. I'm not a psychiatrist but hope that the message of this book will motivate you to make necessary changes in consumption behaviour.

What are your true needs? These will vary from person to person, especially concerning amount, quality, and where the dividing line between need and "nice to have" is drawn. A "one answer fits all" doesn't exist and would be too complex, boring and lengthy to address here. Rather the solution should be your own individual answer to the pre-purchase question; "Do I really need this?"

It might now be a good time to re-visit your personal income and cost analysis to see if that potential reductions column can be added to!

The above refers to all forms of consumption. They probably focus the mind to think along the lines of smaller to medium sized consumer goods (e.g. electronics) but I think a special mention also needs to be made on the two largest consumption items we often make in life, our home and car.

On the house I recommend investing in a roof over your head that fits your true need profile and taste. Unless you're a real estate professional that can read future markets I don't think it's a good idea to mix your home purchase with return on investment objectives. Often the "logic" of making a buck on the private home leads to over-investment in terms of size, location and especially debt. Indeed there is a great tendency to spend beyond the comfortable living needs pushing up debt levels and the exposure and pressure of having to sell at a profit. Whether the debt load and pressure (elements that imprison rather than bring freedom!) "pay-off" is a gamble on often volatile property markets.

Even if there is no investment motive behind a home purchase it still makes sense to buy at, or as close as possible to, the bottom of a property price cycle. Needless to say if the market is close to or at the top of the price cycle stay clear of a purchase and bide time, i.e. rent, or if you already own a home and want to sell then do it now, then rent until you feel the prices for buying are good value again. Needless to say, don't buy or sell life's largest private investment (your home) without doing a lot of homework on the markets, and seeking advice from an *independent* expert.

Concerning the 2nd largest acquisition most people make, the car, if you can control the natural temptation for that dream machine (usually an affliction of the male species) you'll be financially better off. With exceptions as difficult to find as the proverbial needle in the haystack, cars literally waste money. The more you invest and the newer the vehicle the greater the waste. Cars are depreciable consumer goods; they get used up, and usually after 5 years or so lose the bulk of their value through wear and tear as well as technical and market trend obsolescence. The 1st year is a major loss year for a new vehicle, by rule of thumb around 25%. Some makes and models depreciate slower than others but the message stays the same. Without going on about this, my suggestion is to buy used vehicles of a quality make, with limited relative mileage, and in good working condition. A quality vehicle say 3 to 4 years old with 30 000 – 50 000 or less on the clock and which passes a thorough inspection test will serve well for years to come at a fraction of the depreciation loss compared to a new vehicle. The point of buying a quality vehicle supports the length of service, reduced maintenance and, of course, safety aspects!

I'm not saying that life should be ruled by living by the bare essentials budget! We all enjoy the odd luxury and treat. Most of us do tend to earn beyond the bare essentials, so excess earnings should principally be saved (see rule IV). However the odd treat is motivating and adds to the quality of life. I suggest and encourage you plan room in your budget for you and your family to have treats, the odd trip away, that annual holiday, a restaurant outing every now and then.

A point I believe also worthy of note was also passed on to me through my family's Dutch heritage, don't show your wealth. Basically it's neither necessary nor wise to brag about your wealth and possessions, to do so is fruitless and only generates jealously and envy. Anyone who believes that you may have money will be interested in relieving you of your "burden" should the opportunity arise.

To round this discussion off, here are a couple of gems of wisdom from my father which I've always taken heed of:

➢   "you can't take it with you" – referring to the silly obsession
        of people for worldly goods which remain behind when we
        move to our life beyond.

➤ "cheap is expensive" – if you need to purchase something, especially something lasting and functional, best to buy quality that will outlast cheap alternatives many times over.

4. Save regularly, set savings goals, also forced ones, save any extra cash / earnings!

This rule could have been merged with rule #1, it is however a vital stand alone rule in its own right even if you don't have any financial freedom goals. Anyone who lives on the edge, at the maximum of consumption, and who doesn't save will have no reserves at all for the unplanned events in life.

Basically any excess earnings beyond your essentials and your planned treats should be saved. For those on a regular income that excess will tend be periodic and regular, hence it makes sense to save regularly and in consistent amounts. As such it's best to use regular savings plans, and depending on your disciplinary inclinations, it may be best to force your savings for instance by having your bank deduct amounts regularly (at pay time) into your preferred quality savings fund.

After a review of your income and cost analysis and for potential cost savings you'll need to decide how much to save. If you've reached your (real case) optimised income and cost status you'll hopefully have a surplus you'll be able to save regularly. I don't believe in being too tight in budgeting, everything being planned to the last cent, etc. Instead, after leaving some spare room for unforeseen expenses and events decide on your regular savings rate or quota. I suggest you keep your quota a little on the stressed side to keep up a little pressure and discipline to maximize your savings and help realise your goals earlier. The sooner you discipline your savings the sooner you'll realise that more is achievable than you first thought possible, especially over time and with the compound interest effect.

One final principle, save the majority of any unforeseen cash windfall gains, bonuses, tax refunds, etc. It's best to view these "extras" as non-planned nor expected amounts, just pack them away as if they were never there in the first place.

5.   Avoid consumption and speculative debt like the plague!

In line with the discussion on rule III, debt can be like a ball and chain, after a very short and temporary "kick" from your purchase you are left with the burden of having to pay it off. Repeated debt financed purchases only add weight to your ball and chain, so does the interest, all to a point where if you're not careful you'll collapse under the weight of your debt. Put simply, if you can't afford something you want don't buy it on credit. If it's something you need, make do until you have enough saved spare cash to buy it outright. If it's something you want but don't need, that can be fine also, but here, even more so, no credit purchasing.

An even bigger sin is to take on debt finance to undertake speculative investing, be this in shares, property, commodities, or whatever. I know this goes against the grain of many speculators out there but in my rule book it's a 100% absolute no go! If you want to speculate then do so only with any spare cash you may have which, in the worst case, you are prepared to lose. In this book this situation can only arise once your financial freedom goals have been realised.

In chapter 7 you can read more on the topic of speculation, investing and my personal views.

6.   Don't invest your savings in things you don't 100% understand and can't control / manage!

It's not the idea of this book to preach how to invest savings as they accumulate, although aspects of this topic will be discussed in chapter 7. What to do with your saved wealth is one matter; a more important aspect is what not to do with it! The recent Great Recession proved that many investors were shocked to see invested savings and retirement funds devastated by the financial crisis. The point is not that they actually lost wealth, this happens when you invest in equity markets, housing, etc and market bubbles collapse. The issue was that many were caught right off guard, they were shocked, angry, saddened to the point of depression. Not an insignificant number of investors took their own lives. If anyone invests, takes a known and calculated risk but then loses out, it's a shame but at least that person knew what he/she was doing and they very likely won't be wrecked by unforeseen loss. Anyone who invests hard earned savings (for most of us all savings are hard earned) in financial instruments, products, funds, etc without knowing about the workings and up and downsides of what he/she is actually investing in almost deserves to lose his/her savings!

This is hard and I accept a little unfair. Why unfair? Well largely because there is a global financial industry out there that has perfected the art of ripping off an awful lot of unsuspecting savers. Investment product has been pushed at the height of bubbles about to burst, capital life insurance policies sold that don't return more than an average savings book account, funds of mixed asset classes sold with inadequately explained risks, and the list continues. Only recently I had a commercial property fund prospectus on my desk. Without going into detail I literally pulled it apart for misrepresenting profit stream sources and not explaining the main final year exit profit driver which turned out to be a high risk bet no one could assess, but which had been calculated at the maximum optimistic upside in the return numbers. This was after the (maybe only preliminary) brunt of the Great Recession where higher quality standards had been promised by the financial services industry.

The problem here is that not only unsuspecting and financial product illiterate savers are at risk! I had the experience of numerous work colleagues, who indeed are financially literate, who also had fallen into "promising" investments and who had lost out, not to mention countless classic target groups such as lawyers, doctors, etc! Many had invested in products they, well, let's say half understood. One common fault line was often a lack of clear understanding of so called administration and management fee structures, or the illogical thought that tax advantages make for a good investment.

So only invest your hard earned savings in safe and non- speculative instruments you can personally control, fully understand and manage (i.e. no administration or management fees!). My definition of "safe" is where there is no risk of you losing all or some of your capital, total financial system collapses excepted (which we all narrowly escaped through 2008 and early 2009). You have worked, and are working way too hard to risk your saving and financial freedom goals on investments that can tank when markets and economies become unbalanced and go wrong. Such events have always taken place in our economic histories, are now happening with increasing frequencies (especially given excessive public and private leverage and global trade imbalances), and will continue to take place in the future. I will discuss more on these sorts of topics in chapter 7, but for now, in my opinion, the rule stands!

On a closing note, it was this rule that allowed me to realise my freedom goal despite the Great Recession and financial crisis!

7.   Never risk money you can't afford to lose – don't lose!

We just need a short note on this rule as it follows logically from #6. You can't afford to lose money at the best of times, no one wants to lose their cash at any time. You may be in a position to invest in a financial product which you may also fully understand, can manage, and can correctly assess in terms of return and risk. You may be the punting type and be tempted to break out into higher "more decent" returns via a seemingly solid investment opportunity, one however which leaves the realm considered safe (no risk of loss of capital). Great! Are you however, in an honest position to lose all or part of the capital you are planning to invest? If you're not then you're not yet at the stage where you can afford to lose money on an investment punt if things don't run to plan. Such a point in time will vary from person to person and will depend on what their financial freedom definition is, if and when they reach that point.

I've added the text "don't lose" to this rule. It supplements the rule well, but also applies to all investment phases one may be in, be that safe or aggressive where you may be able to afford to lose money should an investment go wrong. At all times avoid losing out on your investments to any material extent. Clawing back such losses is usually arduous, time consuming and painful, also often unlikely! As an example, if you invest say 50 000 in a basket of shares and they slide to 50% of value from the time of your purchase they'll carry a market value of 25 000. Something certainly possible as the last 8 years have shown! The recovery necessary for you to get back to your original investment will be 100%. Such a recovery can take years, if at all. At the time of writing this the Great Recession stock market rally from April to October 2009 managed a recovery of some 50% of the values lost, and this rally was the heaviest, most extreme rally for decades (driven, or at least heavily influenced by, mass cheap liquidity powered by global quantitative easing and without any serious alternative investment opportunities due to historically low interest rates). I'm not sure (but do have my thesis) on what'll happen over the next months and years, but most expert analysis in what I consider to be quality financial press is already calling a stock market (amongst others) bubble that has priced in a level of economic recovery that will never occur, not for the next 5 or more years. As such even the best rally in decades only managed to claw back 50% of the losses made with a good chance that interim gains will be subject to additional corrections, down that is!

In the above example you may have known the ins and outs of your investment, had control (essentially only to buy and sell), and were able to manage your portfolio, but you were not able to prevent a loss of capital due to factors beyond your influence. You may try to read the markets, read up on and follow economic developments, which may help reduce your potential losses of capital, but, neither you nor the best of experts will ever be in a position to be able to read the markets and perfect entry and exit timing to eliminate the risk of capital loss. This was only too evident in the last crash, as with all those that occurred before.

8.   Protect and insure yourself (and family) against major unforeseen risks

There is absolutely no point in building wealth with your savings plans, heading to your financial freedom, if you don't protect your family, self and wealth against unforeseen yet insurable risks!

Some of the classic risks are:

➢   Health and life (covering the income earner and debt coverage, etc,).
➢   Dwelling (fire, lightning, storm, water systems, break-in and vandalism, etc,).
➢   Third party insurance (private, auto, dog, etc,).
➢   Other major assets cover (car, valuables, etc,).
➢   Legal protection.
➢   And other risks applicable to you and your personal circumstances and environment.

To save on these items would be saving at the wrong end. The need to protect against significant risk does not just apply if and when you have wealth; it applies as soon as you are independent and responsible for yourself.

Included below is an insurance risk check list I use to keep tabs on my risks and the status of coverage for each risk. This list forms one of the integral aspects of my own financial planning and management:

Insurances Check List Status xx. x. 2009 (Example only)		Coverage check		Comments
Risk	**Co.**	√	**X**	
Third party risk	xx	√		Raised to xx mio & .....
Dog third party risk	xx	√		
Vehicles	xx	√		
House:				
fire	yy	√		
storm & hail, lightning, etc	yy	√		
vandalism & theft	yy	√		Valuables covered to ca. xxK
contents	xx	√		
water piping	xx	√		
glass	xx	√		
Accident - all members	hg	√		Ends 2xxx - capital + int. ....
Invalidity	zz	√		Includes covered costs up to ca. xxxx p.m. + ...
Legal	ll	√		No restrictions
Health	zz	√		
Bank safe	yy	√		Covered to xxK (xxK in rental price + xxK extra)
Life coverage	hg	√		xxxK risk life policy - x per mth.
Life coverage	kk	√		xxxK capital & payout @yy - .....

9. Pro-actively plan for your finances when you (plan to) stop work!

I have been consistently amazed, or rather have experienced a combination of shock and concern when talking to many people from different countries over the last years on the topic of their end of work financial plans. The messages from such discussions have also been confirmed from numerous articles in the financial, political and social press, also from international sources. I can summarise the basic messages as follows:

➢ End of work financial planning is often limited to half-hearted minimal savings (depending on the country often tax incentivised or regulation required) or life policy plans.

➢ Seldom is independent financial advice sought prior to the decisions on such plans being made.

➢ Serious calculation efforts concerning the cost of living upon retirement and beyond almost never have been adequately attempted nor considered.

➢ Equally the matching or comparison of these with expected / projected wealth and wealth based income hardly takes place or is attempted.

➢ It seems that this phenomenon is particularly prevalent to those in their 30s through 40s (but certainly not only) age groups.

➢ The under 30s are generally aware of the need for such financial planning, but the whole matter is perceived to be too distant and abstract to be of any relevance.

➢ Concerning people in their 30s to 50s there is serious over-reliance on, and expectation from government based pension schemes in those countries where such systems are operating and significant – this is very evident within Germany for instance.

➢ In countries where such state run schemes are not forming the backbone of retirement security there is, I believe, a lack of scrutiny as to the appropriateness of the types of investments being used for retirement funds – this became clearly evident where funds heavily based on share market allocations became severely damaged during the post Lehmann Bros. crash.

➢ Basically significant portions of our population are under investing for retirement, are often investing in ways I wouldn't consider safe (ironic as one would desire retirement funds to be 100% something you can bank on), and are doing this without any proper and transparent idea of their retirement wealth needs. Maybe, people are punting or hoping on higher returns from riskier investment classes for the simple fact that they can't afford, or don't want to afford, conservative lower return retirement funding! Also playing a role here will yet again be the financial industry's desire to play the upside of their financial product returns, which indeed are needed to cover their communicated or hidden servicing costs!

We also need to keep in mind that the above, combined with demographic developments going the wrong way in most Western societies (the serious ageing of the population), as well as the serious increasing burden of public and private finances (with no financial reserves to bring into play), will lead to increasing old age poverty. The sad thing is that there will also be no adequate solid long term solutions in sight. On top, other factors such as rising commodity scarcity and prices, rising environmental issues and costs, will place additional burdens on our post-work financing and standards of living.

Working and planning for your financial freedom (irrespective of your personal definition of your freedom) logically goes hand in hand with planning and pro-actively setting up your finances for retirement. If your interim financial freedom goal is defined as X times annual net pay, your pro-active retirement finance planning will require you to potentially "add on" to that and aim for enough funds to finance your remaining life expectancy adequately from your desired retirement age. For the minority aiming for total financial independence, particularly ahead of the standard retirement age, any need for additional add on planning is logically negligent (all things being equal).

There are essentially two aspects to your financial freedom objectives; (1) achieving financial freedom per your definition applicable for your working life, and (2) equally importantly seeing to your retirement finances so that you'll continue to feel and be financially free from when you cease work. The latter aspect is directly derived from the answer to the mother of all private financial planning questions; the "How much do I need" question!

This question is relevant for the great majority of you, less so for the adequately wealthy, who won't be reading this anyway! A question we have all asked, and will continue to be asking is the question which is directly linked to our inherent wish for financial freedom and peace of mind. It's also a question which can be answered but which also entails challenges and some complications. This is also a question which requires its own chapter.

I invite you to join me in helping you to find your own answer to the question in chapter 5. This will also provide you with your financing goal to allow your pro-active planning for your retirement.

10.   Always ask yourself "what's the worst thing that can happen?" and plan for it – have "plan B" ready!

I couldn't even guess how many times my father said this; "Always ask yourself, what's the worst thing that can happen, plan for that, and if things turn out better then you're fine."

He meant this to apply to all aspects of life, but often his reference related to job and financial matters. This is also very evident in the concept of defining your financial freedom with the essential idea being free from potential threats to your employment and income. Here's an example of some key "what's the worst.." questions which I have asked myself (in so far as they relate to financial matters) with examples of at least part solutions next to the questions in italics:

➤   What if I lose my job? > *Save one or more year's net pay in the bank...*

➤   What if I hit a dead-end in my job and need to "move on"? > *Plan ahead for this and have your strategy for alternatives drawn up and ready to roll...*

➤   What are the risks to the savings / wealth and what if they take place? > *Reduce the risks on how you invest your freedom wealth.*

➤   What if I or someone in the family becomes ill or has an accident? > *Insure these risks as economically as possible or build "rainy day" reserves.*

➢   What if I write-off the car, the heating or washing machine
       breaks down? > *Where sensible insure the car, and in any event*
       regularly set aside capital replacement funds for these types of
       items (the replacement funds should be set aside during the items
       lifetime).

The list can continue endlessly, not just concerning financial matters
but actually in all key matters of life itself. The principle message of
this rule is so wide and applicable to countless experiences in life
that there's no limit to its use. Once you start practising this rule and
the respective solutions you'll experience the freedom it can bring.
Over many years I have found this rule to be a regular bringer of
peace of mind, in small but helpful ways. As can be seen in the
example above it covers everything from daily things that can take
place to serious threats and events that hopefully will be rare, if they
happen at all. Applying this rule is an integral part of finding your
peace of mind and is an important element of your own personal
(financial, but also otherwise) freedom!

The 10 rules are not the be-all and end-all, they are from my
perspective and years of experience, the key rules to keep you on a
solid financial path, a path that if not left can lead to your financial
freedom and peace of mind and hence add significantly to the quality
of your life and the life of your dependents.

5

The "How much do I need?" question

This is probably at least one, if not the, mother of all private finance management questions!

It's a question more or less intensively thought about by the majority as we all speed toward retirement, i.e. "will I have enough when I retire?" It's especially thought about by the upper income earners who may have a chance at early retirement and also by those yearning for freedom from their drudgery at 50 but who objectively remain far from such a goal. It's also thought about by those wealthy enough, but who feel insecure just the same.

I've read numerous private finance books and literature and have noticed that this question has either been knowingly ignored; only minimally or partially answered, or has been conveniently forgotten. Maybe I've decided to take on a task where I can only lose out but am too ignorant to know it? On the other hand I've been active and occupied with exactly this question for years and found my own answer! As such I believe I've identified a classic, maybe perfect, demand and matching supply situation, the demand for an answer to this question is I believe huge, if I can supply a view to the effective means of a solution then wham, I should encounter great interest!

Let's circle back to the concept of relative wealth discussed in chapter 3. Your level of "wealth" is the relation of your net assets and net income compared to your cost of living. If, for example, you have net assets (net meaning after deducting debt) which can be converted to cash over time (liquidated) covering 5 years cost of living then you could be considered comfortably positioned. If the coverage is say 10 years then maybe the term "well off" could be appropriate, and for say 20 or more years the term "wealthy" could well be justified. I'm not aware of an official quantified definition of when one is determined to be wealthy. As mentioned earlier in this book, the cut-off point is often considered by most to be the million mark (globally perceived usually in US dollar terms). A so-called World Wealth Report is produced annually which considers a category of people classified as (and called) "High Net Worth Individuals" (HNWI) starting with investable financial net assets (excluding primary dwelling real estate) of US$1 million. This definition of "wealthy" is not our focus as we are concerned with the amount of net wealth you personally need to feel financially free. Whether that be considered wealthy or not is totally irrelevant. Each individual carries their own personal benchmark determining when they feel financially free, some may use the term wealthy, if so fine, if not, so what?

In chapter 2 we worked on defining your personal understanding of what financial freedom means to you. We also noted that the definition of this freedom can vary over time and indeed move in stages. In your 20s it could be one year's pay in the bank, in your 40s

3 years, and in your 50s it may be enough to adequately bridge you over until, and then supplement, your retirement income whenever that kicks in. I've purposely used the idea of X year's pay in the bank to keep things simple and facilitate a straightforward anchor for the mind, something that will be burnt into the conscience as a simple and effective freedom goal to aim for.

Allow me to fine tune this for the purpose of this chapter to answer the "how much do I need?" question. *How much you'll need refers more to your personal cost of living over the time frame the question is meant to cover* rather than being a function of income and year's pay. This fine point can, and likely will, be significant (in the positive sense) to determining if and when you can achieve your freedom goal, and quantifying / answering the "how much" question! This will particularly be the case the higher your disposable income exceeds your cost of living and the more discipline you command. Put another way, if you earn say net   100 000 a year, with your cost of living at 30 000, and you save the excess 70 000 you'll be on a fast path to financial freedom and reaching your "how much" amount. If you earn net 30 000 you'll need to assess whether your cost of living can be reduced, otherwise the freedom goal will be pushed to the undetermined future. In any event it's the level of wealth that you have, to cover what you need to live, that provides the level of comfort, or freedom feeling.

Let's progress to answer the "how much?" question for you. You'll need to collect some vital information and be clear on your objectives. Here is my (primary) suggested list of what you'll need;

➤   Your goal of financial freedom you'll be aiming for.

➢ Your cost of living over the time frame to be covered.

A less critical secondary list will follow later, but for now this is basically it!

Your goal will require in-depth thought, nothing complicated but you'll need some careful inner reflection to find what provides inner peace of mind. Your cost of living has already been worked out and analysed via the "Personal Income and Cost Analysis" exercise in chapter 3.

I'll now provide you with a straightforward example. Jo aged 30 has his freedom goal set at 2 years net pay in the bank, this is the reserve where he feels he'll have enough to counter his key "what if?" questions. He earns net 50 000 a year. His cost of living is 30 000 per year, but Jo has identified savings potential in the amount of 2 000 from his chapter 3 analysis.

Without much thought Jo associated his 2 year's pay goal sub-consciously with having a mix of 2 years survival reserves and a reserve amount of 100 000 which appeals to him as a nice respectable sum. How much does Jo need to gain his financial freedom?

The answer is variable:

1. 100 000 taking a minimum of 4.55 years (with cost of living savings potential) to 5 years.
2. 60 000 taking 3 years on the 2 X cost of living basis, or
3. 56 000 taking 2.55 years on the 2 X reduced cost of living basis.

The time scale above will also be somewhat shortened due to interest / investment income from savings as they build up. All of this assumes plain sailing and no unforeseen expenditures. It also does not allow for any pay rises, but maybe Jo can simply see this as an automatic compensation for inflation which also hasn't been accounted for on the cost side. Usually things are not black and white, Jo could amend his freedom goal to be the 3rd scenario shown in the list above, once he's reached that he'll likely be well into the practice of saving and he'll likely aim for scenario 2. Continuing in a commendable manner Jo will then aim for scenario 1 and will truly feel (financially) free, having reserves to cover almost 3.6 years and warranting, if not his 3rd, then definitely his 1st bottle of champagne!

As discussed earlier, the definition of financial freedom can be flexible and may evolve over time as you move through the years. In Jo's case he may decide on a phase 2 definition of 4 year's pay near the start of his 40s, feeling the need for more security as he ages and becomes more entrenched / specialised in his job, possibly meaning less flexibility in the labour markets. His "how much?" question will of course require higher reserve answers but he'll be in an excellent position, having more than half of his new goal already set aside around the age of 35.

For the majority of the employed in the west on an average income the above example is, I'm sure you'll agree, worth aiming for. This book is only (unfortunately) applicable for those who are in a situation of being able to set aside enough reserves while still being able to finance their livelihoods. It's the intention of this book however to push the lower cut-off limit for those applicable, hopefully well below the average income thresholds by motivating readers to focus, structure and manage personal finances to aim for financial freedom. I'm glad that this book can address the broad majority of people and hope that this majority can be materially expanded!

At the other end of the income spectrum there are those fortunate enough to be earning well above the average. The people belonging to this group may be professionals, entrepreneurs, merchants, traders, etc who, according to my observations and encounters, think about and yearn for their total financial independence at 50! I'll work further with the example of Jo to address this group but also to address the majority asking what they will need when they reach retirement, say at 65. Whether the target age is 50, 55 or 65, the principle and mechanics used remain the same!

Let's further assume Jo has done well in his career and through the 1st half of his 40s he experienced the right timing and circumstances to move into the fast lane in his career. His pay rose admirably to 100 000 net per annum by the age of 45 and his costs didn't change materially as he had been practicing thrift for some time! The pay and upward climb up the career ladder were great for Jo but also came at a cost. 60 to 80 hour weeks and significant stress started taking their toll on his family life and the first signs of health issues were also surfacing. Jo loved his work, but also realised that a maximum of 10 years could be managed before the price for success would become too high. Consequently Jo decided that at 55 he'd be exiting this pace of work to take a year's break and trip with his wife before seeing what he felt like doing. The key thing for Jo is that he'll be free at 55, meaning he'll be totally financially independent to do what he wants. Jo also decided to make this dream goal his financial freedom goal, something to be focused on and achieved. Indeed, unlike many of his colleagues Jo decided to do more than simply dream, he decided to act and turn it into reality!

What I've labelled the mother of all private financial questions is yet again, for the 3rd time, relevant for Jo again. During the first (two) phases of his freedom goals he was easily able to calculate his "how much" questions as discussed above. For the 3rd calculation the maths and seriousness of the calculation enter totally new dimensions! First of all he's going to base his whole savings structure and strategy to aim and achieve the amount he'll calculate – the amount needs to be substantially accurate as Jo will be working and aiming for it over the next 10 years! Just imagine, he finally reaches his calculated goal after 10 long years, performs his "final act" only to realise that the reserves set aside were off mark. Being out in the cold with miscalculated reserves would NOT be pleasant, not one bit! This of course only applies to the down side, more reserves than needed would be fine, however if the upside miscalculation is overdone, we may have a de-motivated Jo from the onset believing the goal to be too high to reach and ending up not "going for it"!

As you can see the implications and sheer weight of the full financial independence goal calculation are immense. This calculation has an impact on:

➢   The preceding period or years > levels of amounts being set aside over years and the associated sacrifices; the strategy laid out and to be followed not just financially but especially within the career / job (it makes a difference if you plan to stop at 55 or say 65).

➢ The point of time when you "throw the switch" and move into your new free phase in life > at a mature age of 55 leaving a well paid position can mean a one-way move.

➢ The subsequent period of hopefully many free and happy years > you've taken the plunge and now need to rely and be fully confident that your numbers or levels of reserves will indeed carry you to "the end".

This is why I use the term "mother of all private financial questions". So, Jo would like to know if his estimated savings / net wealth goal at 55 will be sufficient at that age to exit his current working situation and rumble to freedom in phase 3, the final round. Jo first needs to set the key parameters for the calculation. In this example I've chosen the following:

➢ At 45 he's managed to set aside some net 300 000 (20 000 per year over 15 years – average interest income on his savings of close to 50 000 were basically absorbed by unforeseen costs over the years) and has achieved his 2nd goal of financial freedom.

➢ Assume an end age of no less than 95 (reaching 85, being healthy and having no funds left would not be a pleasant life's sunset).

➢ End of work at age 55.

➢ As noted before Jo already knows his living costs from his Personal Income and Cost Analysis work. The amount currently reads 30 000 but Jo thinks an average of 35 000 for the next 10 years might be more realistic as his children move through the higher school years and to provide some extra buffer. He also decides to keep the 35 000 consistent, countering any inflation impacts by assuming 0% income growth from his job.

➢   For the purposes of estimating his cost of living from the age of 55 Jo, being prudent, has decided to inflate this number using the 1.5% inflation rate (also compounded) through to when he reaches 55. The amount rounded comes to 41 000 which he'll use in his calculations going forward from the age of 55 when he plans to stop work.

➢   Jo is now in a very good earnings situation at 100 000 net a year. This means he's able to set aside some 65 000 a year (100 000 less 35 000) for the next 10 years – all things remaining constant. Jo expects to set aside some 650 000 over the next 10 years in addition to his current reserves of 300 000. This all should total some 950 000 by the time he reaches 55. Net interest income over 10 years will easily top the 100 000 mark, but Jo adds "only" half of this to the sum, leaving the rest for unforeseen events. With a strong sense of amazement, bordering on light disbelief, Jo sets his total saving at 1 000 000 at age 55.

➢   The 2 dependent children will be either done with tertiary studies or in the workforce latest by the time Jo's 60. According to Jo's Personal Income and Cost Analysis he'll save 38% of his living expenses once the children leave home.

➢   Based on his own research Jo believes that from the age of 85 he and his wife will likely slow down a little and their demands for travel, etc will decline. His research indicates that their living expenses will decline by some 30% from that age.

➢   Jo lives in a historically stable economy with a conservative money supply. The average longer term inflation rate reads 1.5% p.a.

➤   This also implies a somewhat lower average interest rate
      from conservative deposit alternatives with established
      banks at 3% p.a.

➤   Jo decided to buy his house early on in life. Rather than
      paying rent he preferred to pay off his mortgage at moderate
      rates and expects to be debt free by the age of 55. Otherwise
      Jo has no other debt obligations.

➤   Jo decides that his calculations of needed wealth should not
      include two funds which he would like to set separately
      aside for any unforeseen capital expenditure and what he
      calls a "rainy day" fund. The amounts where Jo feels
      comfortable in this respect are 50 000 and 30 000. This
      reduces his total savings estimate at 55 years of age from 1
      000 000 to 920 000.

➤   Jo finally decides to logically include tax in his calculation at
      the known rates, firstly for his current situation, then when
      his dependents leave home, and also at the estimated
      respective rates for his levels of interest income he'll be
      earning. The tax expense numbers will be fed into his
      calculations pretty well near the end when he's fairly sure of
      his estimated wealth from which his interest income will be
      sourced.

Jo essentially has enough data to "test his case" at 55.

What we have to do now is to compare:

1.   The future costs through the ages 55 to 95; with,
2.   The estimated funds and income expected from those funds
       over the same time frame.

This is a straightforward exercise which, if approached in a structured manner, can be completed without too much effort or time. For Jo I've prepared a worksheet table analysis below which I've explained in more detail in the notes below the table:

One-off impacts on model	Age	Year 1 July	Cost of Living	Income from Funds	Tax	Deficit / (Surplus)	Starting Monetary Funds	Inflation Ave int. Inc. / Comments / notes
EXAMPLE Total net wealth needed model J. Blogs							Starting	Inflation 1,50% — Ave int. Inc. 3,00%
50K Capital Expenditure AND 30K "Rainy Day" funds deducted off monetary Assets	55	2019	41.000	27.600	4.140	17.540	920.000	Capex. And Rainy Day funds parked seperately
	56	2020	41.615	27.074	4.061	18.602	902.460	
	57	2021	42.239	26.516	3.977	19.701	883.858	
	58	2022	42.873	25.925	3.889	20.837	864.157	
Kick-in of 38% dependants expenses savings @ age 60	59	2023	43.516	25.300	3.795	22.011	843.320	
	60	2024	27.633	24.639	6.160	9.153	821.309	Tax rate increase after dependents leave house!
	61	2025	28.047	24.365	6.091	9.774	812.156	
	62	2026	28.468	24.071	6.018	10.414	802.382	
				Ages 63 to 70 blended out				
	71	2035	32.550	20.490	5.122	17.183	682.984	
	72	2036	33.038	19.974	3.995	17.059	665.801	Tax rate threshold decline below 20K income
	73	2037	33.534	19.462	3.892	17.964	648.742	
	74	2038	34.037	18.923	3.785	18.898	630.779	
				Ages 75 to 78 blended out				
	79	2043	36.667	15.790	3.158	24.035	526.336	
	80	2044	37.217	15.069	1.507	23.655	502.301	Tax rate threshold decline below 15K income
	81	2045	37.775	14.359	1.436	24.852	478.646	
	82	2046	38.342	13.614	1.361	26.090	453.794	
	83	2047	38.917	12.831	1.283	27.369	427.704	
At age 85 Kick-in of old savings @30%	84	2048	39.501	12.010	1.201	28.692	400.335	
	85	2049	28.065	11.149	1.115	18.031	371.643	
	86	2050	28.486	10.608	1.061	18.939	353.612	
	87	2051	28.914	10.040	1.004	19.877	334.674	
	88	2052	29.347	9.444	0	19.903	314.796	Tax rate threshold decline below 10K income
	89	2053	29.788	8.847	0	20.941	294.893	
	90	2054	30.234	8.219	0	22.016	273.952	Indexed value of House = 647.500
				Ages 91 to 93 blended out				
	94	2058	32.090	5.371	0	26.718	179.042	Reverse mortgage reserve for years after age 95!
	95	2059	32.571	4.570	0	28.001	152.324	
			1.374.909	706.123	126.891		152.324	

Spreadsheet Notes

➢ Jo's accumulated funds read 920 000 (net of his 50 000 capital expenditure and 30 000 rainy day funds).

➢ The spreadsheet calculation starts from 2019.

➢ Living costs read 41 000 in the 1st year.

➢ The living costs have been inflated by the average inflation of 1.5% p.a.

➢ Income on the funds available is calculated at 3% p.a.

➢ Tax expense has been calculated respective to Jo's tax classification and level(s) of income over the years.

➢ The change in total funds at year end is shown as the column "Deficit / Surplus" – cost of living plus tax expenses less income.

➢ At the start of each year total funds are amended for the Deficit or (Surplus) of the preceding year.

➢ The income each year is based on a simplified calculation of 3% of total funds at the start of each year.

➢ The costs of living are corrected at the age of 60 when the children leave home (reduction of 38%) and again at the age of 85 to reflect a fall in costs (estimated at 30%) when Jo and his wife become less demanding concerning travel, entertainment, etc.

➢ At age 95 Jo has around 150 000 reserve funds left. He also has his fully owned private house which has been indexed for inflation up to the year 2059 with an expected value at that time of some 650 000. Should Jo and his wife live beyond 95, statistically unlikely but not to be totally discounted, then they still have their house which, in a worst case situation, could be reverse mortgaged (basically where the house is written over to a bank for the right of the resident ex-owners to live in "their" house till their death and until then receiving agreed cost of living funds from the bank).

This Jo Blogs example is just that, an example, with simplified assumptions and of course fictional data. It is however based on models I use and represents I believe a workable model tool which assists greatly in answering the "how much?" question. As with any example model it will need to be tailored to fit your own personal circumstances and life. Finally such models are susceptible to the quality and accuracy of the data used in them, they are also susceptible to the quality and accuracy of math used, or if performed using an Excel worksheet, then the accuracy and logic of cell formulas used. I strongly recommend when you set up and use such a model that you make a serious effort to check and re-check these factors. I have experienced the need to re-visit my models numerous times for fine tuning on input data and logic, etc.

Having such a model (I recommend using Excel worksheets to allow correction and amendment flexibility) allows changes to be made over time as circumstances alter. The model also serves as a milestone check once you enter your financial independence phase in life, as an example I track my actual fund levels and compare these to the model fund amounts on a half and full year basis, just to make sure the finances are staying on track over time.

Finally for those of you who decide to use such tools I strongly recommend a high level of caution as promoted before in this book especially not forgetting rule nr. 10 (planning also for the worst case and having your plan B ready)! In the above example you'll notice that there is no consideration of any public or company pension schemes. If you have earned guaranteed rights to such a pension(s) then this can be a pleasant additional bonus when it kicks in, and you actually benefit from it. It's up to you to decide your level of caution. Some may choose to include pension rights in their calculations if they deem these to be particularly secure. Others may decide that they wish 100% freedom of dependence on their prior company(s) or government (in the case of a public scheme) and ignore any future pension benefits in their calculations. This latter group will surely take the view that if and when such benefits get paid that they will be indeed an added bonus to be used for that something extra. No matter what your approach to these and other matters, being conservative will protect you from surprises, especially at a phase in life where any significant negative surprises will be most unwelcome after having exited the work place.

To conclude this chapter, no matter what your financial freedom goal, your ability to estimate / calculate how much net wealth is needed is certainly possible. For the majority of readers this is clear. For those who wish to strive for total financial independence the question can also be answered if the approach, as shown above, is structured, focused, and realistic!

6

Your personal financial freedom toolbox

It's one thing to talk about setting savings goals, setting financial freedom goals, etc but the way to manage, monitor and control your living costs so that you will have a realistic chance to meet your goals also needs to be examined! Indeed you don't just want a chance to be able to meet or achieve your financial freedom, you want to be sure. Being confident of being on the right path reinforces your ability to achieve the goals you have set!

In this chapter I'd like to briefly re-cap on those tools already discussed at length and then introduce you to tools you can use daily. In summary there are two groups of tools:

1. Those used for calculations and tracking which have essentially already been presented in this book.
2. Daily use tools used to monitor and control the living costs of everyday life.

The 1st group require effort at the beginning but once set up are easy to maintain and require infrequent maintenance. The 2nd group is easy to set up and easy to use on a daily basis.

Calculation and Tracking Tools

These tools basically form the basis on which one can calculate or monitor the following:

➢ The costs of living and savings / cost reduction potential (Personal Income and Cost Analysis – see chapter 3).

➢ Risk coverage (insurance checklist – refer to chapter 4, rule number 8).

➢ Estimating how much one needs for financial independence (the "How much do I need" question – refer to chapter 5).

There's no need to repeat the purpose and logic behind these tools, this has been done in detail in the chapters referred to above. The nature of the group 1 selected tools presented in this book is of a classic worksheet format. As mentioned before, I suggest you set up your own Excel spreadsheets (alternatively Open Office, or other similar worksheet) files with the content and structure to suit your personal situations. The same calculation basis can be achieved manually (via pen and paper,) however your flexibility to amend, correct and fine tune your data over time will be reduced if using this method.

Daily Use Tools

These tools deal with the monitoring and control of what we spend on a daily basis.

After identifying the level and composition of your cost of living vis-à-vis your net income ("Personal Income and Cost Analysis") and identifying savings potential you're in a position to start monitoring and controlling your costs to make sure you'll achieve your savings goals. The income side of your analysis will usually be set (your income either being fixed or, for variable income, set using the known minimum average) so that the only variable to be managed will be the cost side. It goes without saying that it's the cost side which almost always is the demise of well intended savings goals. As such the control and monitoring of your costs will be crucial to your financial freedom success.

Before we can start monitoring and controlling your costs there are a couple "to do's" which need to be cleared first. These are:

1. Documenting a complete and accurate list of your living costs; and,
2. Grouping your costs according their nature:
    - Regular costs which occur consistently and are fixed in nature.
    - Costs that occur regularly but are variable in nature.
    - Irregular and (logically) variable costs.

You will have completed the 1st task by setting up your Personal Income and Cost Analysis. The 2nd task should also be quick and easy to perform.

Concentrating on the 2nd task, why are we interested in whether costs have a fixed or variable nature, be they regular or not? Basically knowing the nature of costs (as well as the amounts of course) determines whether, and to what extent (how often), you'll need to control and monitor them.

Those *costs that are fixed and regular in nature* are the ones that you can hardly influence, assuming they contain limited or no reduction potential. These costs have to be paid at a fixed level for your current style of living. Examples of such costs can be rent or mortgage payments, utilities (variable but you soon reach a norm average which can be considered fixed), insurances, essential media costs, etc. These costs although being part of your analysis and budgeting process (which will / should be updated at least once a year or when material changes occur) require little monitoring or controlling, what's there to control? Exactly which costs fit this category needs to be decided by each individual as the cost structure profile per person is as individual as that person!

The next group of *costs that are variable and regular in nature* are the costs which you'll need to focus on. These are the costs that have a significant level of discretionary judgement attached to them. They are the costs that are heavily subject to your spending rhythm, spending mood, spending temptations, family and your own "please buy me" pressures. In short these are the costs that can make or break your private financial situation and your savings goals! Examples of these can include the daily / weekly groceries shopping, clothes, going out and entertainment, household and personal consumables (generally smaller non-food purchases of a wide and varying nature but which always pop up, e.g. home office supplies, the odd book, etc,). These are the costs, which because they can literally move from one extreme to the other, need monitoring and controlling.

The same applies to the 3rd category of costs (in the 2nd group), namely *the irregular and variable costs*. These will tend to be the discretionary consumption costs which occur every now and then, e.g. that new electric shaver, the odd kitchen appliance, holidays, the replacement vehicle, house repair or renovation costs, etc. These costs require monitoring and control but not on a daily basis. Capital expenditure items such as cars, house renovation, should be budgeted for in your financial planning and you'll just need to track these items and their costs within your budget. Here the budget, if realistic, should act to contain the amounts you'll be spending as well as the total amounts being spent on discretionary items. Smaller discretionary outlays which are difficult to budget and foresee will have best been planned in your budget via a general expense reserve be it on a weekly, monthly or quarterly basis. These smaller items will need monitoring and controlling as they can be just as potentially destructive (maybe even more so) to any savings plan as the regular / variable costs previously discussed.

In summary we need to regularly monitor and control:

➢   costs that are regular and variable,
➢   discretionary costs that are irregular and variable (apart from major capital items requiring budgetary control only when due).

It is often recommended that to control and monitor costs one should use a household expense ledger or book. While this is a valid suggestion I personally find the idea of entering daily transactions in a book or in a PC Excel spreadsheet rather tedious and prone to longer term failure due to the "nuisance" factor. Basically such a method can be a pain and will hardly motivate you!

As an alternative to the household expense book I developed what I call the "Cash Clock Dashboard". Taking the regular variable costs as an example; let's say my Personal Income and Cost Analysis showed an allowable budget of 300 for groceries, entertainment, apparel, etc for the family on a weekly basis. In this case I decided to make a round dial "clock" with the face showing regular cash markings from 0 to 300, and also allowing negative amounts up to 60, hence the full range being negative 60 to positive 300. I simply added a pointing arm which could rotate to show the cash remaining / spent at any one point in time. At the start of the 1st week the clock's arm is moved to 300 representing the cash available for daily expenses for the week. As the cash gets used the clock's arm is moved back to the new balance of cash available after some has been spent, e.g. the week's groceries for 100 = a cash clock position of 200 remaining.

This works irrespective of whether you use cash or credit card, in the case of cash I recommend withdrawing the week's allocation in one amount giving you a natural "expense brake" which kicks in once you start to see the physical cash depleting. This may be primitive but, I think, an effective cost control reminder. You simply move the clock arm for the amounts you spend and can check if all movements have been taken account of by simply matching the physical cash still available with the clock. In the case of credit card purchases the same mechanism applies whereby you need to make sure you move the clock arm for all card vouchers. Here the physical expense brake is not evident, until the credit card bill rolls in.

Another reason I prefer cash for such expense items is that you're not borrowing money. In my country credit card charges are automatically deducted from the bank account on a monthly basis, in other countries like the US it's common that the credit card institutions allow you to keep the amounts borrowed in debt, incurring interest costs unless you pay the balances off.

Getting back to the cash clock; it can happen that in some weeks more expense is incurred than in other weeks, maybe for items that benefit not just the immediate week but further weeks in the near future. The clock allows a certain extent of "over spending", i.e. the negative scale up to 60. If you need to use the negative side, e.g. say to 50 for a purchase you perform say every 2 weeks this situation is recorded by the clock, meaning that next week your cash allocation is 250 (300 allocated cash less 50 over spent last week) rather than 300. The negative range allows practical flexibility as each week's expenses will not exactly be the same as your budget allocation.

As always in life, the best laid plans can and often do go astray from time to time. Apart from the smaller variations discussed above one can start with the best intentions to keep within the budget and keep those clocks in the positive, but sometimes the odd infrequent and necessary expense may arise which is not covered by the clock allocations allowed and also not covered by the smaller variations on the individual clock. As mentioned before the idea of this whole process is not to allow money and budgets to dictate your life, the process needs to be strict but should not be overdone! There needs to be flexibility so you can exceed the budget without causing any drama.

For larger variations that take more than the weekly / monthly cycles to correct I recommend you also set up an Accumulation Clock. At the end of the week / month you'll have a balanced budget (zero), a net surplus or possibly a net deficit. As mentioned, smaller variations can be "carried" in the clocks themselves and added or deducted from the next week's / month's allocation. Where the variations are larger and can't be balanced (in the case of negative or deficit numbers) or spent (in the case of positive or surplus numbers) within the next week or month, such deficits or surpluses can be shown on the Accumulation Clock. This clock has a larger range of numbers on either side (left for deficit, right for surplus) showing at any one time any accumulated deficit or (hopefully) surplus and will show the need to reign in the "debt" in the case of a deficit over the next weeks. It can of course positively show the amount of spare cash or buffer you may have for that family treat or extra purchase you've been putting off.

What happens if the negative amounts become more regular than you'd like? Well firstly you may have miscalculated your budget meaning your original analysis may be flawed and require correction / research, or, you need to get your expenses better under control! The advantage of the Cash Clock Dashboard is that it is visible to the whole household. Here I recommend that you also explain and agree not only the savings goals, with your partner and family but also explain the purpose and functioning of the cash clock. When you have their "buy-in" then you'll also manage their awareness for cost consciousness and will experience support when some cost cutting becomes necessary! This physically visible attribute of the clocks as opposed to the closed and certainly less visible household expense book is an advantage that shouldn't be underestimated! The main advantage of the Cash Clock Dashboard is that it's very easy to use and to keep up to date.

The cash clock principle can be applied to suit your expense structure(s). For example you may require a clock for your cash purchases and one for non-cash (e.g. credit card, internet, etc buying), maybe one extra for those unforeseen irregular variable expenses at your budgeted allowance (e.g. 150 per month). In any event the working principle of the clock can be applied to your particular needs. What is important is that you cover all of the costs that require monitoring and controlling, i.e. there's no point in controlling your cash and credit card outlays if you forget your occasional cheque purchases! This could actually be dangerous if you believe all expense controls to be working and that you're in budget only to be surprised by a funding hole created by "forgotten" cheque buying.

Finally, to help you visualize a cash clock I've included a graphic image example of a weekly Cash Clock below. My own physical one was made using thin plywood, some paper for the faces, the arms (also plywood) and a small nut and bolt. My dashboard (4 clocks) is tucked away but visible in our kitchen. As mentioned you should develop your own dashboard to suit your circumstances. I found it quite motivating setting up the dashboard and more importantly using it!

7

Supplemental thoughts, opinions and views

Well, what can I say, and where do I start or stop? This is the "catch all" chapter. A chapter to capture all ancillary thoughts, opinions, and views would be beyond the scope of this book, there are however certain aspects I believe need mentioning, namely aspects tied to the question what to do with that accumulated wealth.

This chapter does not provide an investment guide. Nor does it provide the correct answer to the "where to invest?" question! There is no right or wrong answer as the answer(s) depend on the experience, risk, psychology, character, of each individual as well as the volume of your wealth vis-à-vis your commitments and obligations. What I can do however is to share some thoughts on selected investment areas which most people ponder about and which tend to be pushed by the financial industry, and which will also likely impact my own young adult children!

Those areas where I believe I can comment, are:

1.   Shares, the stock market.

2.   Precious metals / currencies.

3.   Banks.

4.   A short exchange on some personal investment experiences.

5.   Thoughts on the diversification of one's wealth.

Shares, the stock market

Concerning shares I've often heard and read that they should make up a significant portion of one's asset allocation, often the advice hovers around the 25% mark. Some of the common arguments read as follows:

➢   To have the chance to participate in the earnings / dividends of enterprises direct.

➢   You'll be inflation protected.

➢   The chance to participate in share price appreciation.

➢   You participate as a part owner in real assets of a live company, land, buildings, patents, people, know-how.

➢   You will have a say in the way "your" company is to be run.

Some "experts" don't even differentiate as to when to buy or not, the implication being you can buy any time. Some even recommend buying at or near the top of the curve situations, along the lines of "it'll always go up" and "there's still upward room to move". Such "advice" was plentiful at the start of the financial and economic crisis in late 2007, and this despite there being ample evidence and commentary coverage that the crisis was well on the way! Needless to say those who followed the fool's market were badly burnt in the subsequent market collapse.

I am not personally anti-shares. I had problems reconciling what my father always said ("only invest in shares if you are fully prepared to lose your money, if you invest in shares then invest only with truly spare money that you don't need") with the views and arguments for shares given above. Personally I think both camps are valid and there is not one right or wrong view. Here are my views which you may find useful for your own assessment:

> Shares do represent an interest in real assets. The implication with such a view is that no matter what happens you'll always have real assets to count on. In my professional career I've seen many companies with real assets which have gone bankrupt or entered receivership / administration. When things go wrong for enterprises, which can and does happen, the so-called real assets no longer encompass the bulk of their value (which derives from their engagement in production). When a business model falters, or if there's mismanagement of the company's resources endangering its profitability, the purpose of the assets will also falter. The logic continues to a point where an enterprise in bankruptcy will have lost most or possibly all of its value, also the value of its so-called real assets (buildings, machines, etc,). The proceeds from the disposal sales of enterprise assets out of bankruptcy are usually a fraction of their original cost or estimated replacement values. This point is however relative, it applies to many (maybe a majority?) listed companies but surely less so to the classic blue chip groups such as Coca Cola, McDonalds, Mercedes, and co.

> Inflation protection works but only if an enterprise remains profitable (in real and not inflated terms that is) and intact.

This also applies to one's ability to participate in enterprise earnings and dividend streams.

➢ Any real ability to have a say in the operations, strategy and leadership or management of "your" company will usually be limited at best. This assumes one holds modest minority share positions.

➢ As seen in the recent Great Recession starting late 2007 shares can lose significant amounts of their market value. Through to March 2009 on most major exchanges globally some 50% value had been wiped out. The recovery required to recoup lost value is some 100%. At the time of writing this book, an amazing 50% gain had been posted in the heaviest rally since World War II, a rally heavily questioned for its appropriateness as macro-economic fundamentals remained weak and the outlook unstable. Irrespective of events in the future, what can be stated for sure is that money invested in shares can indeed be exposed to heavy volatility.

For most normal income earners your savings are hard earned and have been built up over extended periods of time. The question of whether you should invest in shares, how much and in which, can of course only be answered by you. The factors which influence these questions are many, objective as well as subjective in nature. The border between what will be seen as a factual aspect and what as an emotional or gut feeling are rather fluid and subject to individual interpretation. A fast lane gambler will have a contrary view of objective criteria than a fearful and insecure counterpart.

None the less here are some of my own personal views on when it might make sense to invest in the share market:

> In normal economic times shares are a viable alternative for putting your money to productive work and indeed represent an asset class belonging to a portfolio.

> At which point in time one should invest is not easy to determine. Intensive insight will be needed into the macro economic developments (local and international), into the individual markets relevant to the proposed enterprises, into the financial, commercial, and operational standing of the individual companies, into the currency market developments (for investments outside of your living currencies), and political developments can also be of relevance. These and other factors too numerous and requiring separate analysis beyond the focus of this book all require in-depth knowledge, skills, and research to allow informed and hopefully good investment decisions. If you plan to invest in shares; time, know-how, experience and effort will be needed to increase your chances of making sound decisions! There is a mass of literature available on this subject but the use of well regarded and rated independent advisers (generally professionals advising on a time / fee basis, not on a commission basis) is advisable if the sums to be invested warrant the cost.

How often have I experienced people investing in single companies even though they have no hope of reading and understanding the financial statements, and where they have no clue about the industry's functioning let alone the participating company in which they bought shares. These people often based their decisions on tips from friends and colleagues, the press, the prospectuses, the company's own PR machine, as well of course that of the leading consortium banks selling the shares, and so on. Remember rule Nr. VI (don't invest your savings in things you don't 100% understand and can't control / manage!)?

➢ It was my job to go into companies and, with the skills of a qualified accountant and transactions adviser understand and analyse the entities and of course their respective industry. This took weeks if not months, years of experience, deep access to the records and management of the entity, etc. These things per my observations have often not been in existence when people have invested in company shares. Going further, I personally think that those who have made money and who don't belong to the group of the (so called) stock market professions only largely had the privilege of luck in timing and exiting before downward cycles had taken hold, riding positive waves as it were! I for one don't think it wise to invest in this area when you can't assess the investment credentials as a true expert!

➢ It goes without saying that one should buy when the individual share and or markets are down and deemed good value respective to the realistic prospects for the future (not just short term). Generally to buy in times of market hype is not a good idea, indeed to buy when the markets are fearful could be wise.

➢ Only invest with your own money (free excess funds); never finance your share holdings with credit. Leveraged gains can also turn out to be leveraged losses!

➢ Finally I don't have the depth of access to individual entities nor the time to continuously analyse the industries and individual companies. As such when I move into the stock market I'll be investing in market wide indices which cover capital as well as dividend returns, such a market could be for example the German DAX covering the top 30 listed enterprises. The timing of such a move? Only when I believe that there is a good buy, as close as possible to a bargain, will I move in. This call will be based on careful assessment of economic fundamentals in relation to the underlying general value of the shares. This in itself is challenge enough!

For most the ability to perform quality general analysis and specific analysis on individual industries and entities will be limited. No criticism is intended, most are experts in their specific jobs, not in share market investing. For most of you, if you have spare money and wish to diversify, read up on the developments as much as possible and if the investment sums permit, seek some proper independent advice. I suspect you'll have a hard time to truly satisfy rule six and will have to rely on others for your decision, if you're comfortable with that!

Precious metals / currencies

Let's start with precious metals. I'm not an expert in this area but have studied and analysed gold as an investment alternative. In short here is my personal summary of this king of metals:

1. Gold survived as a store of wealth beyond some 5000 years, longer, much longer than any paper (or "Fiat" – Latin meaning something created out of nothing) store of wealth (currencies).

2.   It's the most accepted and popular of precious metals, you
     could say the king of precious metals.

3.   It's portable and can store great amounts of wealth in
     relatively small volumes.

4.   In terms of it's worth I await a grounded and widely
     accepted answer and I've been searching for some years now.
     Basically gold is worth what the markets are willing to pay
     or exchange for it. Its value can vary in a volatile manner,
     albeit in the past the volatility has been driven by central
     bank activity. My personal value measure has generally been
     1 ounce of gold being the equivalent of a good quality suit
     (+/- say 10%). This is however a value measure in a stable
     financial and political world. As such the value you or I
     might be prepared to pay could be higher if we perceive
     rising risks!

5.   Gold does not produce interest or dividend income (for
     normal private mortals), but generally maintains wealth over
     the long term.

6.   It's a classic crisis store of wealth surviving conflict, currency
     crisis, state bankruptcies, inflation, etc.

7.   I personally recommend a certain percentage of one's wealth
     be held in gold, namely around 10%. This as a safety net
     against unforeseen crisis and if purchased at a reasonable
     price you can enjoy capital appreciation. I see gold as a crisis
     store of value and don't trade it as an investment.

8.   In terms of which units to hold I find 1oz. Bullion coins
     practical (Australian Kangaroo, Krugerrand, Maple Leaf,
     American Eagle, etc) as they can be accumulated with
     smaller sums, but represent a classic unit which can be
     bought and sold with ease. For larger value stores I prefer

250 gram and 500 gram bars. The storage of gold is best
managed via an insured safe deposit box with the bank to
which you have easy and safe access.

Whether one should invest in gold, in which amounts and units, etc
is a personal matter. My experiences to date show that everyone you
ask will have a different view on the subject. Hence there will only
be one answer, your own!

Other metals such as silver and platinum can also serve as
alternatives to gold. Silver tends to follow gold as the smaller brother,
platinum, palladium, have a heavier industrial application relevance
than gold. There are pros and cons with these and other alternatives.
I however trust and prefer the long standing king of the metals!

On the subject of currencies I have a simple but straightforward view.
Currency speculation is a no go. I've spoken to the best currency
experts and they themselves admit the opaque and volatile nature
of the area. I recommend that for investing and financing purposes
stick to your own currency, especially if you wish to take on debt
finance.

An exception to this can arise if you have the opportunity to live in
another currency region (e.g. for those with dual nationalities) and
plan to do so. You may then be in a position of having two "living
currencies". Here a rightly timed purchase of the 2nd currency and
investing in that currency will make sense in the amounts your
strategy requires. Importantly I recommend analysis and research of
the relationships of your two currencies to enable you to form a solid
view on fair, favourable and unfavourable exchange rates. As with

all forms of investing the guiding principle of buying low and selling
high apply here also!

Banks

For most normal mortals, we keep the bulk of cash and accumulate
our savings using banks. The financial crisis starting late 2007
suddenly showed the world that a bank is not just a place for your
deposits, and one bank is not the same as the other.

Most, although fewer than before the financial crisis, still view their
deposits with their banks as cash. This is simply wrong. Your
deposits are loans that you make to your bank! As such it pays to
give thought to which bank you choose to use as a store for your cash
wealth. The financial crisis led to a number of large banking
institutions becoming technically bankrupt when their needs for
funding dried up within a short period of time after the collapse of
Lehmann Brothers on 15th September 2008. This collapse signalled a
high point of the fear that a serious number of banks would not be
solvent enough to pay their commitments!

Indeed I remember in the lead-up to this collapse planning
strategic moves for my own wealth for the ever more likely event
of world-wide bank runs. Part of that solution was to diversify
some of the cash across more banks and to make sure that the
banks chosen were solid ultra-conservative institutions that
according to in-depth research had not gambled in markets that
had triggered the crisis in the first place. Another move was to shift
some wealth into gold as the ultimate safe-haven. This took place,

thank goodness, in 2006 when the prices were what I considered "a good buy".

As it turned out the bank runs were avoided on a global basis due to massive government intervention including direct bail-outs of banks and in unprecedented cases states taking control / ownership of them. Governments around the world also decided to guarantee deposit accounts held with banks well beyond normal conditions and limits. This and other supportive events during the lead-up to the financial crisis and the following Great Recession circumvented a repeat of the Great Depression and a total collapse of the financial markets and systems on a global basis. Had such actions not taken place the losers would not just have been the owners of shares, investment funds, etc, but also the average holders of cash deposits in banks, their deposits (which are receivables or claims against their banks) would have become close to or fully worthless over night!

It is to be doubted whether a 2nd wave of bail-outs will follow should a follow-up crisis occur, which is indeed possible as the lessons from the last crisis seem forgotten and as moral hazard takes grip. As such the need to be selective about banks and other institutions you choose to lend your money to will increase. Here are my personal guidelines on the matter:

> Use conservative and well secured / capitalized banks (who are also part of a respected depositors insurance scheme).
> Don't keep all of your cash wealth with one institution.
> Keep a mix of deposits invested at differing time frames, keep enough funds to survive off for the next 12 to 24 months in shorter term deposits for fast access in case of unforeseen

issues or in the case of surprise economic, financial or geo-
political events.

➢   Make sure you can access your cash with short term
    notification.

In addition to the above I confirm my views on the need for a
strategic reserve in gold. As mentioned, in the event of a financial
market meltdown (from which we only just narrowly escaped in
2008) the chances that you can call-in your receivables (deposits)
from your bank(s) in sufficient amounts will be questionable at best!
Don't forget that irrespective of any government or bank depositors'
insurance guarantee, in the case of a full blown bank-run no one will
be able to keep their promise! Some readers will now be thinking
why not just keep cash, as a significant number of the older
generation (at least here in Germany) do. The problem with cash is
that it normally depreciates in value over time with inflation, in other
words you engage in true wealth destruction. Here gold provides a
very real chance to maintain your wealth while also hedging against
potential currency crisis as well.

A short exchange on some personal investment experiences

While following my own rules I haven't invested in anything exotic
during my life. As my modest wealth accumulated I became
increasingly exposed to financial advisers from various institutions
and companies. They all had one goal, to push their finance
investment products down my throat! Herewith a list of some of the
product exposure over the last years with my respective responses;

➤ Capital life insurance > I paid into a so-called dynamic (rising premiums to keep pace with inflation, etc) life policy for about 12 years. The premiums kept rising, slowly but regularly until the point came where I decided to calculate the return on investment. After some simple maths I came to an approximate 3 % p.a. return on the invested funds through to the end of the policy. This could have easily been topped via conservative bank depositing. In other words a low cost simple pure risk life policy (no capital fund building for payout at maturity) and investing the funds at my bank would have covered the life risk and brought better returns. Often the institutions selling such policies for life, accident, etc cover their "costs" with priority rather than attending to any decent returns for the customer! Extreme caution is recommended – check the returns BEFORE you sign up for such products!

➤ Investment funds > I've been approached by numerous "independent advisers" and finance institutions and never touched any of their products. The golden rules of knowing exactly what happens with the funds, control over the funds, etc could not be fulfilled. These "things" were being pushed right up to the start of the financial crisis with the "top expert independent advisers" proclaiming top returns and security like a bank deposit, tax advantages, etc. Needless to say all suffered heavily during the crisis and to date, some of the highly recommended funds were closed or dead. Just recently I had a prospectus on my desk concerning a closed property fund. After some due diligence (my specialisation) I concluded that the document was close to fraudulent, omitting key forecast exit return assumptions, falsifying profitability returns and not listing or adequately explaining key risks. My bank responded to this feedback by stating that it was not relevant for me because the fund had been fully subscribed at the time of my reply. Lucky investors! In conclusion unless you have a professional expert for these types of investments at your side follow the golden rules and stay clear!

➤ Stockbroker "hot tip" shares > in the last few years I've had the pleasure of receiving calls from US Stockbrokers who somehow had my data (partner at a big 4 firm, etc). They all played the same tune, friendly hard pushers of super developing shares in top way-undervalued companies that were about to go through the roof, blah, blah, blah. All came with "introductory offers", just $4000 should be immediately transferred to secure the 1st instalment. After a while, when I saw that all was as said, I could move into larger sums and "kill the markets". These were people I'd never known or met, calling from half a world away, and had the sales hype very well rehearsed so that there was no question that I'd trust them, numerous colleagues of mine had done so! After a while their friendliness had turned sour after my repeated rebuffs. Their investment suggestions also went sour with the onset of the crisis! In conclusion follow the rules and you'll be spared some financially painful moments!

The same has happened with other exotic investment ideas. For example, investing in life policies of prominent people to cash in when they pass away. Just recently I read in the financial press that these investments had turned sour and the investors were co-ordinating their legal action accordingly.

Maybe it's best to conclude this segment not only by re-iterating my personal golden rules but also to recommend a tactical stance. Never be in a rush, never be put under pressure, and never make a fast decision which requires you to shut out any of the rules! Many (not all but unfortunately many) sellers (of not just financial products) try to apply time and lost opportunity pressure. They are also very well and professionally trained to psychologically trap you into a mixture of trust via overwhelming friendliness and familiarity combined with subdued but powerful guilt feelings which arise if you don't move their way. Always be the calm calculated one who will think about things in time and who will call them IF YOU are interested, or the simple "no" is also very effective!

Thoughts on the diversification of one's wealth

Even though many (also good) financial authors advise how to diversify one's wealth portfolio, into which asset classes and within which proportions, I will not! It took me a while to realise why I haven't been following their advice, even of those few who I dearly respect. The simple answer is that they've been advising a mix which entail areas where I'm either not in a position to have full knowledge and confidence in the investment field, or the timing is wrong (no "good buy" situation yet) or the "must invest in these areas" fields are simply not compatible with my financial make-up or character.

Diversification is logical and important, but a one size fits all solution is not possible. The whole idea of this book and the underlying principle is to build your wealth and protect / grow it in a safe manner that you understand and where you can sleep peacefully at

Appendices

27 years rat race – adventures, lessons learnt and motivation to become financially free

I admit I had the type of family upbringing everyone longs for, an intact family, stable and loving parents, two brothers and two sisters, a dog and a cat, all in a house full of character and the continuous adventure that a family of 7 brings. It was a protected and rather comfortable time right through to the end of my tertiary studies; college (uni) was just 5 minutes drive from home. Appreciation for all this only really came when I was about 35 through a gradual realisation that my "normal world" was in fact abnormal compared to the real norm out there.

In 1982 I left the home nest at the age of 21 and left a country town of 58,000 heading for the "big smoke", Melbourne, with a population of 4 million. All seemed set to go, the 1st job with one of the so called "Big 8" (in the 2000s later to be known as the "Big 4") accounting / auditing firms, a 15 year old car, a few hundred dollars and a bank card, and very importantly, the 1st apartment. We, my college friend Rod who landed a job with a competing firm and his girl friend, decided to club together for an apartment which was great for the budget and provided company.

Yes, this was when real life took off. The first job was at A$12 500 (gross) a year, indeed a modest sum for the auditing profession, but we were grateful as not so long ago the pay was zero, it being a honour and privilege to start in the public accounting profession. We also started work with the statistic well parked in our minds that the training costs to get our useless theory-filled uni grad "egg heads" up to an elite professional standard and qualified was half a million dollars per employee. And, you know what? I never regretted this move! But there was more than the job, it was the first free place to live, inclusive almost hippy type conditions, it was also most importantly, having full responsibility for my own actions and setting the course, albeit with minimal conscience thought, for my entire future. My mate Rod (and those I came to know later) were not any different I must add, except that Rod was possessed with making as much money as possible and simultaneously not spending a cent. True optimisation one could say, although other terms also exist. Anyway, after about a week of living-in, the 1st day at work was just a weekend away.

The first day, although somewhat blurred, did leave some lasting impressions! It started with a crash course in navigating the pathetic (back then) public rail transport system. I only lived one suburb away from the CBD (Central Business District), the direct line distance from South Yarra to the CBD of Melbourne must have been no more than 5 km. The rail company back then however had the organisational talent to manage an average of 45 minutes to master that 5km. No stops, correction, plenty of stops but no stations between my suburb and the city centre. It was disgusting but soon became the norm of travel whenever I had "non-productive" time scheduled for the office as opposed to so called "chargeable" time at the clients.

Getting back to the first day I finally made it to the main train station called Flinders street. It was about 8:20am as I stepped out of the 1920s red train carriage (and seemingly never maintained or upgraded since) and proceeded into an ever thicker blob of commuters. The station was packed, being fed by streams of people departing the trains just arrived, being compressed in its inners, and then being spewed out of the main entrance. I was also spewed out, walked a block into the CBD and then crossed the road. I stopped and remained standing still for some time while looking back toward the station. With the eyes of a country upbringing I simply observed the streams of working commuters for some minutes, and was shocked and uneasy. I saw myself, cloned thousands fold, gray or dark blue suits, clean shaven, walking without the hint of a smile, all seemingly with the same brief case, all heading into a selection of business towers. Even the weather, which was great that day, didn't help. These "me clones" all of a sudden had sheep heads (I guess a country life vision) and all were herding together like well behaved live stock, and the most amazing thing, all at free will!

Strange, but this uneasy feeling was more than just a first work day sentiment, it was actually disturbing. This feeling said loud and clear, "this, my friend is not you, nor will it ever be". It spoke silently but clearly, "let's see how long you will last in this." And, this feeling spoke the truth, a truth I would learn to cover up in the pursuit of other "more important" goals contradictory to my true self.

The timing of my employment contract was standard, i.e. post summer break to coincide with the start of the 30th June financial reporting season and consequential audit work required on company accounts. My new colleagues and I had to be trained and worked in before being unleashed on our audit clients as "Associate" (assistant). A long haul awaited us! Three levels or ranks as Associate (A1, A2, A3) then 3 as Senior Associate (SA 1-3), Supervisor (which could take up to 2 years), Assistant Manager (grades 1 and 2), Manager (often 2 years), Senior Manager, and then, maybe (meaning probably not) partner. Partner was "God", the goal of all goals, the "you've made it"! It was however so far away that other goals got in the way.

I had my first real working life experience before those other goals became relevant. The year in which I started work just happened to be the start of a heavy recession. Soon I would learn that my firm had lost a major audit client to a price dumping competitor, and elsewhere not just audit but also advisory services budgets were being cut significantly.

My first client was unforgettable, a ship maintenance and engineering firm in the Melbourne dockyards. Females were banned from visiting the client, something I would later well understand. Just a week before my client's introductory tour the crane driver had been shot dead. The finance personnel upon whom I depended for documentation and answers to audit enquiries were very special indeed. Apart from just being extremely coarse in speech and action, they also insisted on shortened working days, every day that was, for the whole duration of the audit. The mornings were somewhat productive but then came the lunch times, every day in the pub, the food was fine, the beers too. After the 3 hour working lunches the rest of the day was a write-off. Yes, this was the deal to get through the audit, which we actually did. They even paid for the inefficiency, but what a start to the career, fun but somehow worrying.

Back to the recession! After some 6 months I was sitting in the office filling in time with self learning and networking, meaning begging for any work from underutilized managers and supervisors. This went on for weeks. My skills in photo-copying and filing also became well developed. Talk began of a "hit list", and indeed young colleagues soon started to disappear. The hit list phase went on for about 6 weeks and ended, it would seem, with me. Late Friday afternoon I was called into the head of personnel office. He explained the obvious lack of business and then confirmed my fears – yes, I was out.

Very embarrassingly I could hardly hold back the tears as I headed to a vacant manager's office to close the door, regain some form of regular breathing again, and call my saving anchor in life, my father. He was furious, claiming breach of contract, unfair play, and especially the lost chance to enter the post graduate public accounting programme, basically meaning a claim for damages on a ruined future career. A law suit was on the table that weekend but never had to be activated. The following Monday I was called into the personnel partner's office only to hear that any retrenchment programme was off, that there never was a hit list and that the firm looked forward to having me serve them on a continuing basis. It didn't take long to get my head down again and concentrate on the next goals.

Lesson learnt

Don't bank on your plans as being certain, nor take initial progress as a guarantee that the out come is a given surety. There are factors out there that one can't steer nor compensate.

The next move was passing the rigorous post grad-exams (expected to be completed usually within 2 to 4 years), you had 2 shots, then you're out, not just of the chance to obtain the title, but also from the firm! Studying for this was basically masochistic, one worked a full day, learnt often in groups in the firm or at the institute, studied weekends, engaged in interim module tests often with "character building" setbacks, and all to face the pass or die exams over 2 full days at the end. The unique combination of work plus study had some heavy side effects, e.g. the time I managed 5 car accidents within 24 hours due to lack of sleep. If one managed the title, it was then interesting to learn that if you were still a senior manager at the age of 35, and not on guaranteed path to partner, then it would be time to leave.

Don't get me wrong, this wasn't all torture nor all negative. My admiration and respect for the profession, of which I am still proudly a member, remains fully intact. One advantage of a stringent and highly structured programme was that its self-accelerating momentum sucked you in and became almost self-fulfilling, not bad for a young graduate seeking orientation. Not to mention the great colleagues with whom one learnt in groups, through thick and thin. It was all intensive but worth it, it was clean, productive and led to higher things, so we all did it. Some made it, and some close colleagues didn't, not due to a lack of intelligence nor effort either.

I managed the exams at my first shot, just as well as I was already in Holland ready to start what was originally planned as a 6 month secondment with the same firm. International transferability was, and remains, a major strength of such firms and my profession!

Holland was fantastic. Apart from not learning the language (my firm's official language was English and the Dutch spoke it effortlessly) I dived into a world of crazy but fun ex-pats, exotic characters and cultures and all but boring partners, especially one from Bangladesh. I was about to learn a lot about business practices and culture from the very able Dutch.

Six months turned out to be thirty. After about two years the learning curve was flatter, I realised that good ex-pat friends also had their own plans and started leaving, and I had become trapped in an ever turning cycle of work, pubs with the lads, the same social events with the firm over and over again, all fun for a while but it also started to become suffocating. I also started to realise something was wrong when I would regularly go to the office on Sundays. At least I had real work to finish, unlike a number of colleagues who went in just to have their time accounts register their presence on such days, all to "further their career". Month 24 was somewhat critical, I got restless and was about to make another character building mistake.

My wife and I decided to give Germany a go. Without securing an alternative job I resigned and embarked on a ski tour combined with a job interview at a small operation in south Germany. The firm was I thought active in audit related financial matters but turned out to be a sales operation for financial products, with my perceived role being the "sales guy" for Holland. The next surprise, pay was close to 100% commission driven, if you can sell then good, if not bad luck, basically zero security in all aspects. Well what a mess, being a salesman was not my thing. This was not good, no job and a botched exit due to a total lack of research and many other factors which could be summed up as "immaturity".

At least the ski break was fun. I'd just become unemployed without a plan B but didn't really care, probably because I was qualified, experienced and young, hence in the true Australian manner, "don't worry mate, she'll be right". The same tactical blunder 10 years later would have induced more panic than anything. Back in Holland I crawled back to my exotic partner, embarrassed and feeling like a complete idiot, asking for my old job back, he agreed without hesitation, sigh!

After another six months we landed in Germany after all. My firm had arranged a transfer to their office in Frankfurt. Why didn't I just enquire about this possibility direct rather than making an idiot of myself? To this day I don't have an answer!

Lesson learnt

If you plan a major move in your career or job don't quit prematurely, find a true alternative that is solid and fits your strategy, and research this alternative properly. Also, if you've had a longer and trusted relationship with your current firm try approaching them 1st before making any drastic moves, if they value you this won't be a tactical error, and they may just be able to help. Another lesson learnt, why the rush? Anything done in a rush usually backfires.

The "3rd phase" Germany would prove to be the greatest learning experience of all, a 22 year phase and the inspiration for this book. The 1st five months at the Frankfurt firm were a shock. Newly promoted to Supervisor which meant something in Holland turned out to mean nothing in Frankfurt. This combined with a dreary atmosphere and a lack of ex-pat powered dynamic made me feel as though I'd fallen into a funeral home rather than my next station for the next couple of years. I gave my new work base a chance but soon realised that no one was interested in my position, track record nor the 5 year's experience with the group in Australia and Holland. I was, or felt like, an outsider.

Joint audit client contact with a South African working for the competition opened a new opportunity. We talked about my situation and he promptly offered to arrange an interview with a large, very traditional, German, audit firm. The interview ran well, and I soon resigned from my old firm which I no longer recognised since being in Germany and took a plunge into a true culture shock. English was rare at the new firm, and all my presumptions of a typical German organisation seemed confirmed, hierarchical, rather stiff, very formal, and something I hadn't really thought about, all communication in German, yes I agree, how ignorant! What I did find amazing though was an uncanny but pleasant feeling of honest interest and welcome radiating from my new colleagues.

It was this feeling of warm interest that motivated me to stick it out. Without any previous schooling in German I had no choice but to learn the language on site, being surrounded by the language was tiring but the best thing that could have happened. Within 6 months I was actually conversing with the locals, even with the clients, my

German reading also was at a level appropriate for the job, wow, it felt a little like those films where a young child goes to Japan learning the culture and language from base zero.

I quickly established a good relationship with my new employer. The next seven years were steady as she goes. Here I got to know the "real Germans", appreciate their culture and learnt to put many of the generalisations and clichés to rest. My firm had a different grade ranking structure to the last employer, the path up was also slower and not so easy for a "misfit" like me, but I think I learnt so much more in this environment than would have been possible in a more internationally driven group. It was around 1995 that things became a lot more dynamic, this was the time that my firm, some close colleagues, and I discovered that one could make money out of company takeover transactions.

> **Lesson learnt**
> Particularly while you're still young (but also later) take a risk if it means breaking out of a dead end. A dead end may be secure and a comfortable situation you know, but a dead end is what it is. You may survive for quite some time, but the deeper you go you'll also seal your fate of ending up miserable. You'll be so far down the path you'll have no rations left for an about face.

The formation of a super troop called "Transaction Support" or abbreviated simply TS happened around 1995. The few close colleagues, who had joined forces on previous advisory projects supporting clients in their takeovers, and I formed an unofficial group, much to the suspicion of our responsible bosses. The traditional and core business was after all audit and tax and not some form of mutated service mix dependant on the takeover whims of the odd client. Not to mention the unprecedented and difficult to assess risk to which we may be exposing the firm.

We, I mean the mini group TS, went our way. Some support became available from those who saw that money was to be made. We wanted to be snazzy, we were amongst the very first (for our environment) who used mobile phones, they were almost the size of bricks and just as heavy but we were proud. Yes mobiles and "prescribed" energy foods and drinks were our companions into the dynamic world of company takeovers. Some three years later we were a group of about 12 but you could double that if you included those who helped out occasionally. We had improved recognition in the firm and the additional revenues were becoming more welcome as time raced on.

The TS projects became larger and more complex, the number of nights and early shifts became more numerous and "normal". By 1998 we were viewed upon as being dynamic, but also nuts! A bunch of people who willingly worked under permanent stress, normally around 12 to 18 hours a day and who had to deal with pleasant clients but often aggressive and increasingly arrogant (don't ask me why) bankers responsible for financing the deals. It was also not proven, and indeed was seen as sceptical, that such a path would ever lead to the magical admission in the partner club. This I was to realise when my own highly expected admission fell flat on its face. I'll never forget the body language of the partner who dashed my hopes. Before he had even broken the news he was half cowering under his desk after being surprised by my extremely sour and apparently aggressive face, something a company training psychiatrist would tell me a few years later could indeed become a fearful weapon, something "perfect" for the business world. It was this face that would sometimes unfortunately and unwillingly terrorise my family as I became slowly but increasingly more aggressive in what I prefer to call my sub-character.

> **Lesson learnt**
> If you want to make a particular goal, especially a very difficult one, do your homework on ALL the factors you need to get right and managed. I simply believed that hard work and technical success would pave the way to promotion, wrong! Any larger move within any (I'll bet almost any) organisation means tactical play, getting key sponsor relationships set up and working. It also means assessing the time needed for this, in any event double the time you'll first plan. Unfortunately it also means being tactical (but fair) in dealing with your opponents and competition.

In the 1st attempt I didn't make it to partner in 1998. Bad timing, well I thought so, as this was also the year of the big merger, not just a merger with a competing firm, no, more than that, one with my previous employer, who also had a TS group. Their TS group was double the size and was led by a very (putting it mildly) aggressive guy who saw no reason for our group's existence, as it soon became obvious that we were mere plebs and amateurs in his eyes.

I had learnt the last lesson well and the merger was opportune after all. The typical infighting that accompanies most mergers or takeovers was especially prevalent within our small group. We were the first to experience the power struggles and would also be the first to exit such struggles, like a heavy thunder storm the infighting was to be severe but at least fast and cleansing. Our side of the group and our leaders suddenly saw the need to establish a "balance of power" between the warring factions, and that our side was too light to achieve such a balance. It was also fascinating to see how all of a sudden this business had become one of focus, yes relevant after all and worth protecting and positioning.

Mid-1999 I was admitted to the club, against the will of the opposing leadership. The year of merger and the following 2 years turned out to be political hell. It was only the long battle to make the club that kept me going. This period of repression, even the word terror comes to mind, was about to end. The maker of hell was not only seen as such from my perspective but fortunately also by a number of our firm's senior partners. It was amazing to observe how a technically brilliant partner colleague not only had it in for me but also continuously attacked the authority and standing of a number of senior leaders, amongst them my key club case sponsor! Two things became his undoing, (1) the ever zealous aggressive push for power which always triggers dangerous reactions combined with, (2) an unbelievable level of arrogance which was excreted in every gesture and also verbally.

My opponent had lost any sense of instinct and had no antenna for the reactions that his style of inter-personal talent were causing. He just didn't stop. One arrogant gesture or comment after the next, diplomacy in the quest for more power was completely foreign, the body language (widely acknowledged as being by far the most important form of communication) patronised people in the most extreme form. This phenomenon was not just sporadic but continuous, and the guy didn't realise the amount of damage he was causing, meaning damage to his own future within the firm. After a sideways "promotion" to an, in his view, insulting area of responsibility he left the firm. This was the start of a calmer and constructive phase for our group.

> **Lesson learnt**
>
> Your position in any organisation is also a function of inter-personal skills. You may be technically brilliant, an excellent salesperson, etc but if you cancel these positives via an inability to "get along" (meaning showing respect and understanding) with others you'll likely end up worse off. This can maybe best be summed up with these words of wisdom from a wonderful former neighbour of mine ".. with your hat raised you'll always get along well in life ..."

The demand for advice on company takeover transactions was high. On average I managed approximately 10 deals a year. The deals differed in size but commonly were for transaction values in the tens to hundreds of millions of euros. I even had a few deals running into the billions. This was definitely the up-side of the job; it was indeed exciting, high profile and international. Always meeting new people, new industries and companies, new mentalities and business philosophies, new challenges, and continuously having the feeling that I was always in demand and looked up to. This was a job at the very high end of our profession, high earnings, high risk, highly demanding, pure stress but also kind of fun. This was a job in the fast lane, a job that one could perform, it was often said, for about 10 years max. The 1st seven to eight years fitted this perspective view, hard, crazy work but fun.

By the end of a total of 13 years in this business I would be personally looking back at some 150+ transactions. The last of these years however were about to bring new issues and challenges.

Being "drugged" or "high" from life in the fast lane kept one issue well shrouded. I came to slowly realise that I and indeed a number of my colleagues had fallen into a career trap.

One of these traps related to the highly specialised path that we had taken, without boring you with the technical details our product or service offering was very technical and for the 1st 7 odd years fairly scarce and hence well in demand. This all meant good revenues and profits; so much so that we became possessed with the direction we had taken and stayed on the path for years. Our product however became more commoditized over time, the competition grew, and the service provided became less scarce, so much so that even our clients started to set up their own internal groups to perform the same work. We saw all of this coming but failed to spot the trap I'll call "over specialisation".

I realised what had happened over a relaxing chat with Paul, a head hunter I had known for years. That evening we exchanged views on the economy, markets, etc. On the second beer, more as a joke than anything, I asked Paul what he could do with a 44 year-old partner with a reputable 8 or more years experience in my service line and some 24 years in the profession. I was expecting a laugh and a list of clients just waiting for the chance to grab such a bundle of expertise and talent. He took a slow mouth full of the amber elixir, placed his glass with precision back on its beer mat, looked seriously at me and said, "nothing"! His next sentence came over like that of a wise elder speaking to an over-confident, almost matured friend who still had some of life's lessons to learn. "You're too specialised in what you do, you've been doing your type of work too long, you've been with the same company way too long, and on top your age is also an issue. Just stick to what you're doing and enjoy your beer".

I was shocked.

Paul went on to explain what the financial and corporate labour markets were after. Essentially people under 35, dynamic and with multi task experience. This meant people who perform work in one field for say a maximum of 3 years, then hop positions (better employers) getting into new fields, and so on. The profile described would have been an unreliable "job hopper" to my understanding, but no, this was the profile of the future. Yes, forget it you middle-aged partner, you're there to stay, a good position, well paid, etc so why be shocked, be grateful and relax. No matter how true this may have been, I was trapped it would seem. As mentioned before I wasn't the only one, there were also colleagues, just as trapped and worse still not, nor ever to be, members of the club! Yes, it would appear that I or rather we had made a tactical error in our almost over-engineered career planning. That evening, and for the days thereafter, I learnt another lesson.

Lesson learnt

At least once a year perform a career path review. Map

out what you've been doing, how long, etc, and reconcile
this with the employment market trends and demands.
Don't use your own interpretation of these trends or
demands, you may be, shall we say, "out of touch".
Research what's in demand out there via reliable sources,
maybe best of all by talking to a few good head hunters.
If you discover a miss-match, reset your goals and career
path strategy.

I quickly accepted my fate. This wasn't after all so hard to do. I was
after all in the club, had made it to the top of the hill, was earning
well, and was secure, well I thought so anyway.

It became quickly obvious that in order to remain in the club ever
increasing revenues had to be generated and this in a market where
the competition was becoming extremely aggressive. Falling margins
and prices, ever aggressive clients who thrived on the near begging
antics of our "beloved" competition, and our ever eroding claim of
exclusivity in our service offering, all meant an exponentially falling
job fun factor.

On top of all this the climate within a firm hardly improves when
the market in which it operates becomes worse. So be it, one falls
into a sandwich situation, slogging around in the external market to
barely keep the revenues in line with a paradoxical rising budget,
and having to increasingly defend one's own position while others
saw away on the legs of your office chair. An ugly monster's head
had re-surfaced, that despicable saddening aspect of human
behaviour I had had the pleasure of getting to know during the club
entry battle some 8 years ago. This time however the reason to fight

wasn't the holy-grail club membership, this time it was just having the right to stay in position, a right to stay under pressure, keep up that increasing negative stress and ever more frequent medical check-ups. What a great feeling! Being frustrated by an increasing proportion of literally unbearable clients where I truly came to understand the now widely publicised and criticised vertical free fall in business moral standards. Defending the status quo of a once "cosy" position had simply become a tiring pain.

One doesn't need to be a rocket scientist to guess the end of this story. I strategically put up with the situation for a few more years. On the radio there was a chart hit titled "sick and tired", it was catchy and dealt more with a broken love situation, but my interpretation was work related, yes indeed I was "sick and tired of being sick and tired". I spent the last 2 years intensively planning my exit. This meant running post-exit (financial resource) budget numbers through one spreadsheet after the next, running hundreds of scenarios through my mind during breakfast, showering, exercising, while driving to work and seeing clients, and at the day's end and evening. I tried to switch this stuff off during weekends, to little avail however.

I won't bore you with explicit exit details, some of them also for legal reasons, but I will mention the key factors that drove my personal strategy and planning. From my past job I've come to appreciate using bullet point text structures, so here are some of the key factors;

➤   I clearly defined what my life's goals were and what freedom meant to me.

➤   I then assessed where I stood in relation to these goals, and

> what it would take to achieve them and become free.
> ➢ Defining and quantifying the financial resources needed to match my goals and freedom was the next step.
> ➢ I had to then define a realistic time line, in my personal case this being almost exclusively driven by financial aspects.
> ➢ Given the situation I was in I had to then superimpose the above goals and financial needs over my job situation and circumstances.
> ➢ This involved mapping out the time line, financial mile stones, and optimal tactical moves during the rest of my career.

The master plan, put in simplistic and broad terms, was to have the financial firepower to be able to move into a new phase in life by exiting my job and living simply yet comfortably. Living a slower paced life in which I could pursue the things I always wanted to do, without the chains of having to serve others. To have simply continued would have in all likelihood led to significant material wealth, though at the cost of the other goals and freedom. It would have also likely cost my health and the total absence from the few years left of my children's remaining time at home, more years of job related despair for my wife, these amongst other things. The price of simply continuing versus my goals and definition of freedom would have been too high.

The plan was implemented with a level of precision, dedication, and outwardly calm nerves that you can only attain via years of "training" in the environments I had been exposed to. At a strategically planned point of time the master plan was activated and executed, like a piece of surgery. After following my plan, achieving one mile stone after the next, I was able to realise a successful, harmonious and positive exit from my job.

To be explicit, there was a detailed master plan developed over the last few years, however, it was preceded by a number of years strict adherence to a specific financial philosophy and specific key rules which were also a part of a long term "freedom plan". The absence of such a philosophy and rules would have kept the final master plan a dream, nothing more.

Enough biography! I truly wish you Annika and Stefan success and fun in achieving your financial freedom! The same goes of course to anyone who reads this book.

Epilogue

One year hence

It took longer than I thought to come from the fast lane to a much slower but wonderful winding country road, months actually. The change was abrupt and sudden and it took time to grasp that the goals set over the last years had actually been achieved, all of a sudden!

What can I report on my experiences over the past year? Here are some aspects that may be of interest to those of you planning a similar move:

➢ It took time to trust my own financial plan numbers and calculations. This may sound strange coming from someone of my background but it's what I experienced. It's one thing to have the best of financial and budgetary plans, they may be as conservative as possible, with back-up reserves, but validation is truly only possible when the plans become activated and switch from theory to "live"! Everything worked out, but being a suspicious and cautious type of person I still find myself checking – well, every now and then anyway.

➢ Many colleagues were quite envious, not in the negative

sense but rather in the "I wish it could be me too", sense. I often heard that with time I'd become restless and would surely feel increasingly like the roof would be falling on my head. Well, I can't confirm this!

The mind works with logic but the emotional and subjective acceptance of such a brutal change takes time and patience. Now after the big move and months of what I term de-toxication I can confirm that the decision was the right one. It is now with a fresh view on life, new energy, having dropped the chains of suppression moving from a "have to" to a "want to" mode, yes achieving true freedom, that I am able to realise one of my goals, writing this book.

Using my newly won freedom it's now time to help others less fortunate in our society. I also plan to continue writing!